CESAR PELLI

Selected and Current Works

THE MASTER ARCHITECT SERIES

CESAR PELLI

Selected and Current Works

Introduction by Michael J. Crosbie
A Conversation with Cesar Pelli

First published in Australia in 1993 by
The Images Publishing Group Pty Ltd
ACN 059 734 431
6 Bastow Place, Mulgrave, Victoria 3170
Telephone (61 3) 561 5544 Facsimile (61 3) 561 4860

National Library of Australia Cataloguing-in-Publication Data

    Pelli, Cesar.
       Cesar Pelli: selected and current works.

       Bibliography.
       Includes index.
       ISBN 1 875498 13 3
       Master Architect Series ISSN 1320 7253

       1. Pelli, Cesar. 2. Architecture, Modern—20th century—United States.
       3. Architecture, American. 4. Architects—United States;
       I. Title. (Series: Master architect series).

720.92

Edited by Stephen Dobney
Designed by The Graphic Image Studio Pty Ltd,
Mulgrave, Australia
Printed by Southbank Pacific Pty Ltd,
Fishermans Bend, Australia

Contents

Introduction

A Conversation with Cesar Pelli
By Michael J. Crosbie

*The name Pelli is also the Italian word for "skins".
So it is wholly appropriate that this monograph is organized according to the skins with which Cesar Pelli has clad his buildings. The skin, for Pelli, is the primary mode for expressing the system of building. While other reviews of Pelli's works have focused on them as purely aesthetic objects, this monograph presents the architecture as the architect thinks about it: as an expression of construction technique, a generator of urban life, the result of a carefully designed process for making buildings in the late 20th century.
The work process of this prodigious firm has been the subject of as much design attention as the work itself, and Pelli's partner, Fred Clarke, joins the conversation to explain the work methods that are particular to Cesar Pelli & Associates.*

CROSBIE How did you come to study architecture in the United States, after your education in Argentina?

PELLI I grew up very much as an Argentinian, and I realized much later that my family was atypical. We had fewer ties than traditional Argentinian families. My mother has been all her life very active in teaching, lecturing and writing, and we had a home environment that looked as much toward the rest of the world, particularly Europe, as to Argentina. This was even more so with Diana—my wife's—family, who were Europeans, who had come to Argentina in the late 1930s because of the Civil War in Spain. Both her parents also taught. In 1950 I graduated, was working, and had just married, but was restless, needing to see more. I applied to study abroad and one day this envelope came with a ticket to study in the United States at the University of Illinois. "Where is Illinois", my mother asked. "South of Chicago!" We were to come for nine months and we had every intention of returning to Argentina. But after nine months we had a son, we had debts, and both Diana and I had offers to teach at the University of Illinois. We stayed another year, after which I was offered a job with Eero Saarinen. And before we knew it, we were Americans.

CROSBIE How valuable to you were those early years with Saarinen?

PELLI There were two critical periods in my formation: the first was my schooling at the University of Tucuman, which was extraordinary, with great intellectual effervescence. At Illinois, there was no comparison. I was much better prepared than anyone there. I had a solid understanding of the principles of the Modern movement and I knew how to use theoretical constructs to design with—that's perhaps why my professor was impressed with me and recommended me to his friend John Dinkeloo, who offered me a job with Saarinen. This was most important in my development. It is one thing to get trained in a school where you learn what architecture is about, but another to become an architect. In one you learn theories about swimming, but in the other you have to jump in the water and swim and are properly coached. This is what happened with Saarinen. Good, sometimes great architecture was being done there and we were part of it. All that it takes to produce good architecture was there, open to our eyes. It was being created by Saarinen's efforts, which were visible to us, and by our own efforts, which we could interpret as we wished. Usually great architecture is seen as this thing that mysteriously happens, produced by extraordinary beings. The truth is that it is done by means that everyone has, some more than others.

CROSBIE	What did you learn about the process of architecture?
PELLI	I carry a number of things that I learned from Saarinen, of course transformed to the circumstances of today and my personality. One commonality is the open process. Occasionally Eero would come with sketches from home, with a complete *parti* for a building. I remember that every time he did that, things did not go so well and the process was harder. But when the design process was in the open, it was infinitely richer, and it was easier for the whole team to carry it further. So I never come with sketches from home, or do them alone in my office. I will conceive ideas, but I make sure that the first time I put them on paper I do so with my team around me. As I start working, they may say, "Hey, you forgot that we don't own that piece of land," or whatever. From the beginning, the design is informed by the intelligence of everyone participating, and by their research.

At Saarinen we had an open process, and we also used models. The regular use of large-scale models developed during the design for the TWA Terminal at JFK Airport in New York. Eero had designed the terminal before I was part of the team. He had been working on it for about a year. Then a model was built to present to the client, who approved it for working drawings. The next day Saarinen called the client to tell them that he did not like how the design had come out, and he wanted an extra year. He got it, and we started over. What happened was that when Eero saw in three dimensions forms that looked good in drawings, he realized that some were terribly awkward. I was asked to resolve a problem with the legs of the shells. I developed the sculptural forms that were built. Then I was put in charge of the design team and a whole new aesthetic approach grew. We ended up building a very large, very crude model and testing everything in model form. The extraordinary value of models as a tool for designing became obvious to me. They are an impartial, objective way of looking at architecture. If I start drawing something and it doesn't look good, sometimes by just thickening a couple of lines the same drawing looks very good, but the architecture hasn't changed—just the thickness of the lines in the drawing. Models are built following a rather rigid convention. They don't tell you everything, but they are much closer approximations than drawings. I can study them together with my team and share them with my clients. Models are also efficient. I make a few comments and give direction. I go away, the team works very hard, and the next morning I can review the models again and quickly understand what the aesthetic or functional issues are and decide on the best direction for the design to take. |
CROSBIE	You also use models to test three or four ideas simultaneously.
PELLI	Correct. We also did that with Eero. The way we draw with the stabilo pencils also came from that office, starting with Eliel Saarinen through Eero. Just about everyone in our office can draw that way. I like the technique because it expresses volume and it renders buildings in a tangible way. I must confess that we use it less now since computers.
CROSBIE	Do you see similarities in how you use models and renderings in design, and the way you use computers?
PELLI	The model tells us more than a computer drawing does. A computer screen is two dimensional. But in some ways we use a similar process. We also study a number of alternatives using computer drawings. My concern is that with a computer it is easy to produce too many alternatives in a short amount of time.

CROSBIE	Too much choice?
PELLI	No, the problem is not too much choice. The problem is that it allows the architect not to think. That's bad. In developing three alternatives, one has to think hard about it. Two or three alternatives can be very good ones. But with the computer, it is possible to produce a thousand thoughtless alternatives, and that's no good at all. That's the danger. Just producing and choosing alternatives is not design. Choosing from alternatives is one specific aspect to the design process, but it is not the design process. What directs the design is an intention. If you have an intention, you can choose options that will take you closer to your objective. But only if your objective is extremely clear. If you don't know where you're going in a design, just choosing will get you nowhere. There are a thousand steps in the design process, and a thousand choices at each step. So you can become thoroughly lost by just choosing. It's the intention that matters. The architectural intention includes artistic objectives, functional objectives, social objectives, the whole complex world of architecture.
CROSBIE	So you have a clear intention in most cases?
PELLI	Yes.
CROSBIE	How do you arrive at that?

PELLI	Our first steps are always the same. We start by analyzing the problem, talking with our clients, visiting the site, walking around the city to see the character of the buildings and understand the tradition of the area, studying the program, and analyzing the budget. We also build a model of the site and its adjacent buildings. Then we build a couple of models of what we call "dumb" schemes—very obvious and simple massings—just to have an idea of what happens when you put something that big in that place. At this point one has to make an intellectual and subjective leap. Given all of the factors of the project, I usually see two or three ways to respond to these conditions that will give us the best possible building. Then we test these alternatives, again in a crude form, until I sense that one idea is a better response, will be the better building, and has greater artistic potentials. You should notice that I do not start with sketches or design ideas. I always wait until I have a thorough understanding of the problem before I start conceiving solutions or forms. In this way we have no false starts and the design responds from the beginning to all the circumstances of the problem. Almost always I will try to put into words what it is that we are seeking. So each scheme has, from the beginning, a theoretical backbone—something that the whole team can refer to as they are seeking to solve minor or secondary problems, or to develop other elements. The purpose is always articulated.
CROSBIE	At what point do you articulate it?
PELLI	As early as possible. Most of the time, if the project is clear, I'm able to articulate an intention very early on. It gets adjusted as we go, and elaborated upon. Often we'll discover secondary but important possibilities that were not apparent at the beginning, and I count on those opportunities appearing as the project develops.

CROSBIE   Do you articulate the purpose verbally or graphically?

PELLI   Both. I do very simple drawings, enough to communicate the idea. Sometimes I'll develop an idea over a drawing with trace. If I can articulate it verbally, I'd rather do it that way. I draw only if I need to.

CROSBIE   So this is a conversation that goes on with everyone on the team?

PELLI   Yes. I try to involve everyone on the team. When we have client presentations we try to include as many members of the team as possible. Everybody is part of the process and should hear it first-hand. Designers working with me are not my "hands", they are my collaborators.

CROSBIE   This sounds similar to the way a design studio works in architecture school. Is this a technique developed through teaching, and as Dean at Yale's architecture school?

PELLI   Of course. But in school the purpose is to encourage each student to seek his or her vision of the problem. Here, the purpose of the team is to help me develop my vision of the problem. The teaching–learning atmosphere is the same as in a design studio, but the primary purpose is quite different. Teaching helps you to articulate, helps you to listen. But as a teacher you shouldn't interject your vision of the problem. When teaching I offer guidance but no solutions. In the office, I do the reverse but in a similar context.

CROSBIE   Your work has incorporated many different materials over the years. How do you arrive at the choice of a material— how do you appraise its potential power in a project? What makes it the right choice?

PELLI   From the beginning of my practice I wanted to understand and express the nature of today's buildings. Contemporary buildings are containers of space and, given our building technology and standards, these containers need to be tight, efficiently sealed envelopes. This is totally unlike traditional masonry architecture. I wanted the maximum artistic expression of these qualities, and San Bernardino City Hall is probably the clearest of all of the buildings that I have done in expressing this idea. The City Hall is a very didactic, polemical design. The Pacific Design Center is in a similar category. I became interested in going beyond that—keeping the same conceptual basis, but exploring it in different ways. The only way to achieve a consistent, total envelope is to do it in glass. Because buildings need windows, there is a certain percentage of the skin that has to be glass. If you want the building to be one material, the only choice you have is glass. And the San Bernardino City Hall is one of the clearest expressions of that potential. The American Embassy in Tokyo required that the walls be concrete for security reasons. How do you do this and at the same time express the taut enclosure? I had to rethink the problem to be able to include concrete and other materials, like stone, which today can be a very thin veneer, as we used it at the World Financial Center. I have been moving over the years to be more inclusive—if I can use a Charles Moore term—in the use of materials and in exploiting their expressive potentials, while maintaining the intellectual integrity of their relationship to the nature of contemporary buildings.

The San Bernardino City Hall pointed up a weakness of my early approach. It was architecturally correct and extremely well received by the press and my peers, but in my mind something was wrong with it. It was not doing what it should be doing for the city. What was the problem? It became clearer to me when I started to design buildings in much more critical contexts. The real test was Herring Hall at Rice University in Houston. When I went to the interviews, the building committee said that they had been wrestling with the fact that nobody liked the newer buildings on campus. But everybody liked the older, Ralph Adams Cram buildings. They asked me if I could design a building more like those. I told them that I agreed with their observations, but I didn't know if I could do it. Those are historical imitations, and that I wouldn't do. Herring Hall helped to resolve in my mind what had been up till then an unresolved conflict. Why is it that so many buildings that are so well received by the architecture community are not accepted by the public at large, are not enjoyed, and do not fit in their surroundings? These are essential objectives that any good architecture must achieve. Part of the solution was that some of my aesthetic predispositions had to give. The key to my being able to design responsive and responsible buildings while remaining faithful to our Modern condition is in the consistent relationship between the aesthetic system and the nature of the construction technology and systems with which we build. It's not that we have to express every line in a truss, but there has to be a correlation: a non-bearing wall should not look like a bearing wall. This has helped give intellectual continuity to my work.

We happen to live in a period in which a number of materials are available. There's nothing wrong with brick, stainless steel, or stone—why should I artificially limit my palette to make my work appear consistent, if I believe that the consistency between my projects is secondary? The consistency between a building and the place it is in, or with its purpose—those are very real and essential conditions. My approach is what is constant. If I build an art gallery it has a certain character. A gas station, or a factory, or a church, all should be different. If I build in New Haven for Yale, it's one kind of building, and if I build in Tokyo for NTT it's a different kind of building. Using every time the same aesthetic system with the same materials is a conceit. But it is a conceit strongly supported and promoted by the press, the critics, and the academics. Aesthetic consistency is easy to recognize and understand. Architects who have been able to maintain a consistent aesthetic approach can have their buildings identified with a recognizable image—it's a Richard Meier, a Frank Gehry, a Norman Foster, or a Michael Graves. For me it is more important to connect with the purpose of the building and the real place where the building is. This means that the images of my buildings must vary to suit their specific circumstances.

CROSBIE   That was also true of Eero's work.

PELLI   Yes, it was very true of Eero. When I was with him
I thought that was one of Eero's weaknesses—that he did
not have a recognizable style. He said he was looking for
a style for the job. A style does not interest me, but the
basic intention is the same. I was fortunate that in my
formative years I was not trained to believe that aesthetic
consistency is an essential goal in an architect's work.
As you know, the vision of almost every young architect
is distorted with this presumption. Architecture is the art
that should change more according to the circumstances,
more than painting or sculpture. I believe that we have
been misjudging the practice of the art of architecture,
because architectural criticism has been overly affected
by painting theory and criticism. Over the last 100 years
painting has been the dominant art and its theories and
biases have been extended to architecture.
But architecture doesn't fit. It has very little to do with
painting. It is a very different art and there are a thousand
other dimensions to architecture—social, economic,
physical—that have nothing to do with painting analysis,
but it continues to affect the way we discuss and judge
buildings and architects.

CROSBIE   These discussions are framed by critics who were trained
in art history, not architecture. Getting back to our
discussion of materials—glass, aluminum or stainless
steel seem right for what you want to achieve in your
architecture: the expression of a tight envelope.

PELLI   They are materials that express most clearly what I believe
to be the nature of architecture today. This is one of the
yardsticks that I use to evaluate the choice of materials:
the appropriate expression of the nature of contemporary
construction. In the case of multi-story buildings it is the
thin envelope. That's the way I believe that we will keep
on building, so it is essential not only for my architecture
but for architecture at large that we get on with the task
of figuring out how to do an architecture that
is expressive, versatile, and suitable to all the tasks
of this marvelous art, and consistent with the way we build.
The ancient forms of architecture have all come from
a particular way of building. Arches, corbels, pediments,
quoins—all of these architectural elements grew naturally
from bearing stone construction and are completely
consistent with the way we used to build, but don't
any more.

CROSBIE   Many of your projects play important urbanistic roles: projects such as the Commons in Columbus and the World Financial Center in New York. How do these buildings energize a city?

PELLI   Wonderful cities, wonderful urban places, are so because they have been able to achieve a certain density, a certain intensity of potentials, that make it wonderful to be there. It is much better, of course, when this happens in beautiful spaces with handsome proportions. Whenever one has the opportunity to accommodate and strengthen the forces that bring people together in the city, that interests me very much. Those qualities are at the heart of what makes our built environments good or bad, and they are more important than a building's aesthetics. There are places where the buildings are not extraordinary, but they make great cities. Paris is a good example. There are several great buildings in Paris, but what makes this city wonderful are all of those ordinary, good buildings that create spaces for activities and intense urban life. The urban places, the streets, the plazas are more important than any one building.

CROSBIE   How did you adapt these lessons to your own architecture?

PELLI   The precedent for the Winter Garden at the World Financial Center in New York was the Commons of Columbus, Indiana. They are representations of a new building type. I call them Public Halls or Public Rooms. They are public living rooms for the project and the city, and the number of different things that happen in them is extraordinary. These Public Halls are spaces that are centers of activity, focuses of urban life. The Commons is clearly the center of public life in Columbus. Irwin Miller of Columbus had asked me to design a small downtown shopping center. Miller wanted this project to bring downtown Columbus back to life. But a shopping center won't do that. The idea for the Commons was to create a space on the downtown street as a covered extension of sidewalk life at one end of the shopping center, not as part of it. This is not a mall. It is more like a downtown living room. You enter from the sidewalk on Washington Street, and it has its own life so it can function separately from the shopping center. Miller asked what would happen in this space. I told him that I wanted it to function for late 20th century America like a piazza functioned for 17th century Italy. Mostly it would be a great place where people would come, read the paper, have a cup of coffee, meet with friends. But occasionally something will happen there that will bring in people from the whole town. They have hundreds of such events every year. The Public Hall has to be downtown, because this is the only place that can bring all citizens together. People of all economic and social strata gather there, and it adds an essential dimension to the life of Columbus.

We just finished our third Urban Room at the NationsBank Corporate Center in Charlotte, North Carolina. It is already changing the nature of downtown Charlotte. None of these halls was in the program given by the clients. In all three cases I proposed them and, to my delight, they were accepted and built.

CROSBIE   Fred, how did the firm's organization of collaborating with other architecture firms on large projects evolve?

CLARKE   Our process for collaborating began when the firm had very few people and, for pragmatic reasons, we joined with other firms in going after large projects.
This also coincided with our developer clients' interests in combining design firms, for marketing and other reasons, with solid technical firms. Now, after almost 16 years and more than 70 collaborations with other architects, our collaborative design process and products have become very thorough and complete. This is not design as you would understand it in school. In addition to schematics and design development we work through all construction documents and follow the project through construction.

This is also distinct from what is sometimes described as "design consultation", which some well-known architects have done. Our collaborative design process is something we do for about half of our projects—for the very largest projects and those that are distant from New Haven. But the other half of the practice provides full services in the way a more traditional architectural practice would. This is a distinction that one always has to make because, in general, people like to associate us only with design. The collaborative work has informed the traditional in the sense that the refined level of our communication with our associate architect in terms of design ideas and intent has had a significant impact on the quality and comprehensiveness of our full-service drawings and specifications. The level of our design development drawings, outline specifications and follow-through during construction administration is extraordinary.

CROSBIE   Was this a matter of amplifying what you had done while providing just design services, or did it require a new approach to construction documents?

CLARKE   They are two very different processes.

PELLI   The reason we separate them is because the workplace culture necessary today to do good design is different to the culture you need to do good working drawings. To do good design you need an office that is loosely structured, with an emphasis on creativity. People are more independent. If you run a large working drawing department in this way, you will either go broke or mistakes will be made. In a well-run working drawing department, people work regular hours and the tables are neat and clean. A design studio is rather messy.

When you have these two cultures together, there are
two solutions to house them. One is to separate the
two activities as departments usually on different floors.
The other way is to organize the whole firm around
the characteristics of a good working drawing department
with regular hours and neat desks. This system is easy
to manage and the livelihood of the firm is more at stake
in what happens in the final working drawings.
The problem is that the whole firm becomes tight,
and the creative juices cease to flow. But we can run
our firm as loose as we wish, like a small, creative *atelier*,
and we associate with firms that run very tight, neat shops.
If the two cultures are combined in one firm, there are
usually extraordinary jealousies, but when they are in two
firms, there's no conflict. The primary reason for splitting
the work is to maintain the open, loose environment
to work on design. The second reason is to maintain
a smaller size firm. When we do our own working
drawings on small institutional projects, we do them
a bit looser. Two people do all the drawings.
And the construction documents for these projects are
produced by people who were on the team from the start
of design. There's no division. When you have a team
of 15 people, each one drawing a piece of a large
building, you can't allow any looseness or something
will fall through the cracks.

CLARKE   Though our teams are vertically integrated, with
            designers, technical people and a management person
            all mixed together, culturally it's an extension of the
            design studio. This is what makes our way of doing full
            services a bit different. Culturally, the ethos and the
            values instilled in the team spring from the design-team
            background.

CROSBIE   Beyond the preservation of the design culture,
            and the ability to do large projects with a small office
            if you associate, what are the architectural advantages
            of collaborating?

CLARKE   The advantages to our clients of having two independent
            firms with independent assignments is that the project
            gets thorough scrutiny. When a project is done by a single
            firm, there's a tendency to let decisions drift until late
            in the process, which you can't do if you're associating.
            There's also a tendency to favor one aspect of the
            process—technical or design. When two firms are
            working on a single project, there is a devotion to
            your speciality and assignment. A project under these
            circumstances probably gets more service and scrutiny
            than a project done by a single firm.

PELLI   We don't associate with the same firm all the time.
            We select the best firm for each project. We associate with
            local firms because they know the people and the process,
            and are there to service the client. We will associate with
            different firms depending on the building type, so we can
            get the best team of people possible. You cannot have that
            in a single office.

CLARKE   You're free to think about the very best possible approach
            to getting the work done. You can choose the best
            consultants, the best associates, the best collaborators
            and, within your own office, the best team for that project.

CROSBIE   In collaborations, how do you maintain the amount
            of control over details?

CLARKE   Our design development drawings and outline
            specifications are essentially preliminary working
            drawings. Quite often, the list of drawings done

and the list of issues considered in design development is worked backward from the most important ones during working drawings. In effect you develop the working drawings process in its skeletal form and apply it to design development. Communication is crucial in collaborations, and you're always thinking ahead about what are the most important issues for us to communicate. In that regard we simply don't address many things because they aren't important to the work that we're doing. We're also attentive to how you draw it and communicate it in graphic terms, and how our staff works with the staff of the other architecture firm.

In terms of protecting the quality of the details throughout the process, you need to know what's important to set priorities. There are many details in a building that are really not important to us aesthetically. They are extremely important in terms of keeping water out, or cold air out and warm air in, but they're not necessarily what we concern ourselves with. The collaborating firm does that. Our staff has been educated to find what are the most important issues, and then to chase those thoroughly.

CROSBIE   And what do those issues tend to be?

CLARKE   Anything having a visual affect, which is a broad statement. This will include key exterior wall details, how materials transition one to the other, floor and ceiling patterns, how light switches and thermostats are placed on the wall, handrails, and much more.

PELLI   If we have developed a detail that we love, but the associate architect convinces us that this detail will lead to water penetration or staining, then we'll redesign it to fulfill the technical, pragmatic goals. Most of the firms that we've associated with once will call us later when they have a client who wants a high design. We get a fair number of clients through other architects.

CLARKE   There's also the issue of follow-through. During the design phase the collaborating firm is with us all the way. By the time we end design development there shouldn't be a single surprise to the other architect. Conversely, we follow working drawings and construction administration all the way through. Quite often our team size at the end of design development will reduce by only 10 or 15 per cent. We know that clients don't like for us to disappear, and we don't like the idea of losing control of our aspect of the project. Consequently, with us shepherding our work and the technical architect his, the buildings are very carefully put together.

PELLI   Sometimes we will use a material new to us because it appears most suitable. But we make sure that we acquire a good understanding of how the material behaves aesthetically, in the construction processes, and in cost. We may approach a material new for us, such as stainless steel, rather tentatively. But once we understand it, we become very knowledgeable in what that material can and cannot do technically and aesthetically. There's a great temptation to use only materials that one has mastered: once you know brick, you do everything in brick. That's too easy. It's wonderful to discover new materials. And a new material forces me to reconsider to some extent the nature of architecture. It keeps me fresh. One dies artistically when one ceases to question oneself.

Michael J. Crosbie is an architect and a Senior Editor of Progressive Architecture, *who has written extensively on architecture in the USA.*

Selected and Current Works

Urban Nucleus

Design/Completion 1965/
Sunset Mountain Park
Santa Monica Mountains, Los Angeles, California
Sunset International Petroleum Corporation
Reinforced concrete

Centered on a protruding spur, the Urban Nucleus juts out toward a view of the Pacific Ocean and terraces radially downhill with one long arm following the line of a connecting ridge. The urban unit follows the natural forms and will not change the shape or scale of the hills. The project consists of 7,100 residential units zoned for an irregularly bounded 3,500-acre parcel of rugged undeveloped mountain terrain.

Housing units are terraced on a series of concrete platforms down the hillside. The central, topmost portion contains the social and commercial core. Inclined elevators link the center with the residential units.

1

1   Aerial view of model
2   Section

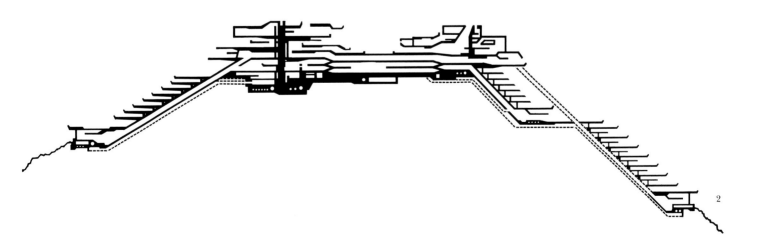

2

Glass

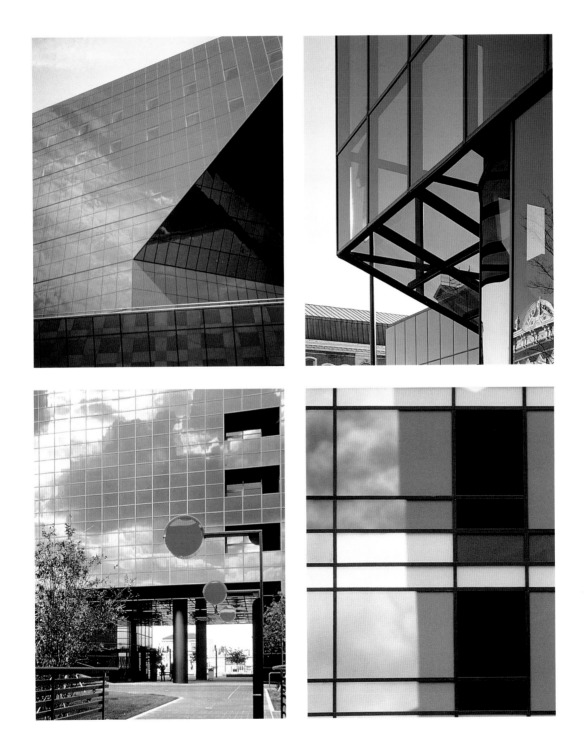

San Bernardino City Hall

Design/Completion 1969/1972
San Bernardino, California
City of San Bernardino and the City Redevelopment Agency
112,500 square feet
Reinforced concrete
Tinted bronze glass windows and dark bronze structural
glass spandrels

Located 50 miles east of Los Angeles, the
San Bernardino City Hall is at the center
of a downtown renewal project including
convention facilities, private office buildings
and a major civic plaza and parking.
The six-story building provides space for the
city's administrative departments, including
the council chamber. Service elements
(elevators, rest rooms, mechanical services)
are on the sun-exposed south side and
offices on the north side.

The City Hall is a strong sculpted form,
completely enclosed in glass.

1

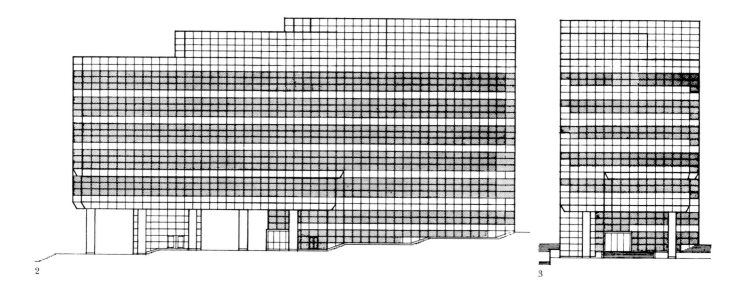

2

3

4

1   View of building from the southeast
2   North elevation
3   East elevation
4   Exterior wall
5   Ground-level plan
6   Upper-level plan

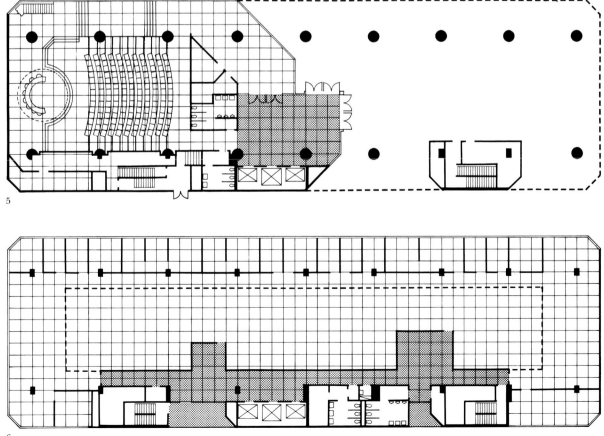

5

6

UN City

Design/Completion 1969/
Vienna, Austria
City of Vienna, Austria
4,000,000 square feet
Steel
Glass: clear and coated

The design team won first prize in the
international competition for the design
of this International Organizations'
Headquarters and Conference Center
in Vienna. The program provides
headquarters offices for six international
organizations, and 15 conference and
assembly halls. Offices are housed in seven
towers ranging from 12 to 38 stories.

UN City was designed to change and
to grow—elements can be changed
or expanded at any stage of construction,
or after they are built. The entry concourse
can grow or be connected to new spaces.

1

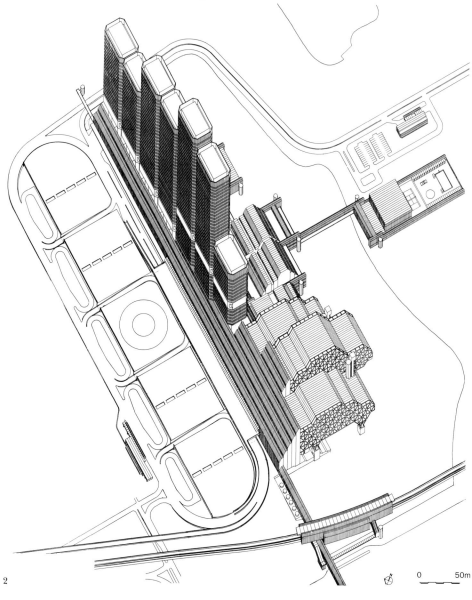

1   View northwest
2   Axonometric
3   West elevation
4   East elevation
5   South elevation

2

0   50m

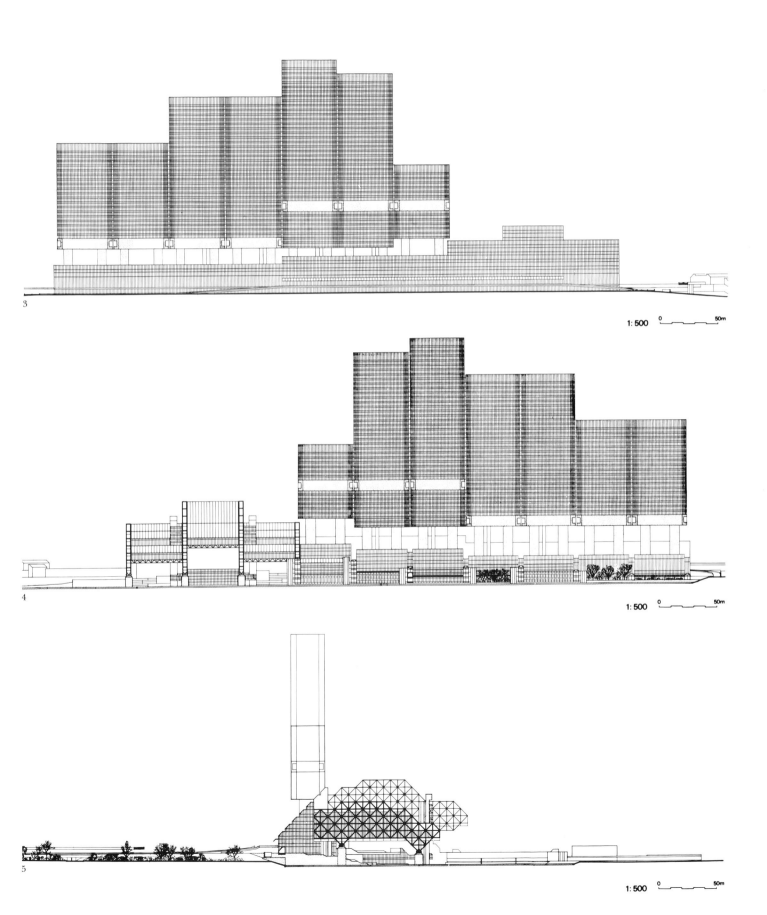

3

1:500 0 ___ 50m

4

1:500 0 ___ 50m

5

1:500 0 ___ 50m

Commons of Columbus

Design/Completion 1970/1973
Columbus, Indiana
Irwin Management Company Inc.
240,000 square feet
Exposed steel trusses support curtain wall frames in steel tubing
Gray-brown ceramic and vision-glass curtain wall

The Commons and Courthouse Center
are two distinct buildings situated
on an 11.9-acre two-block urban renewal
site in the center of downtown Columbus.
A public space owned by the City
of Columbus, the Commons accommodates
a playground, exhibition space, cafeteria
and sitting areas and is part of a successful
downtown revitalization effort.
The Commons functions as a public room,
attracting people of all ages. It is enlivened
by Jean Tinguely's 30-foot kinetic sculpture,
Chaos No. 1, installed at the center
of the space.

1

2   3

1 View from Washington Street
2 Interior view with Chaos No.1 by Jean Tinguely
3 Night view of interior
4 Washington Street view with Courthouse
5 Perspective section of Commons

4

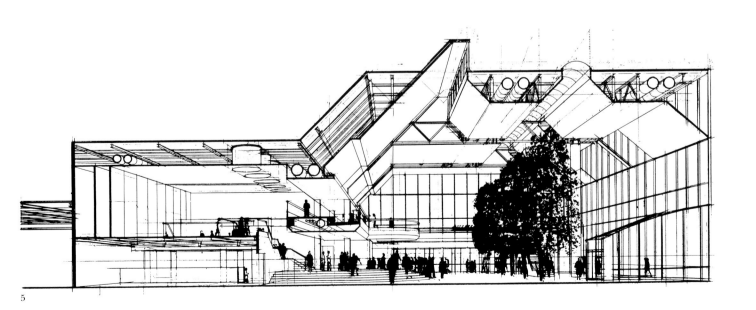

5

Niagara Falls Winter Garden

Design/Completion 1975/1977
Niagara Falls, New York
Niagara Falls Urban Renewal Agency
50,000 square feet
Concrete columns supporting steel lattice frame
Steel, clear tempered and laminated glass, aluminum curtain wall

The glass-enclosed Winter Garden, 120 feet in height, is the focal point of the Rainbow Center in downtown Niagara Falls. Its removable panels on the north and south sides enable retail shops, restaurants and hotels to open directly into the landscaped space. A system of bridges, elevators and stairs encourages vertical and horizontal movement throughout the Winter Garden. The Winter Garden is landscaped with a ground cover of vines and shrubs, palms and broadleaf evergreen trees reaching 40 feet in height, in addition to brick and stone walks and cascading pools.

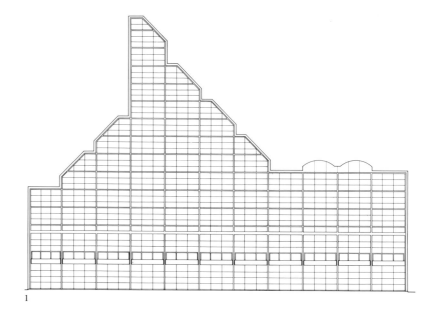

1

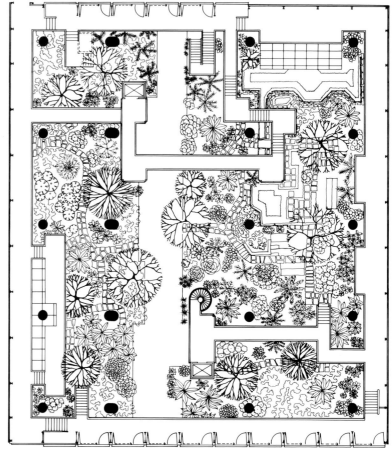

1   West elevation
2   Ground-floor plan
3   View from the west
4   View of Winter Garden, showing landscaping
5   Night view of west elevation

2

N   20'/6m

28

3

4

5

The Museum of Modern Art
Gallery Expansion and Renovation

Design/Completion 1977/1984
New York, New York
The Museum of Modern Art and the Trust for Cultural Resources
of the City of New York
384,000 square feet
Reinforced concrete frame
Multi-colored ceramic glass curtain wall with clear and tinted
vision glass and eleven shades of spandrel glass, restored
marble walls

The expansion more than doubled the size
of existing gallery space, increased the size
of curatorial departments, added an
auditorium, two restaurants and a
bookstore. The Museum also sought to
reduce operating deficits by building a
residential tower using the air rights over
the new galleries. Vertical movement is
achieved primarily by means of a series
of escalators enclosed in a glass hall, which
opens new views of the Museum garden,
54th Street and parts of uptown Manhattan.

The rebuilt facade on 53rd Street, designed
by Philip Goodwin and Edward Durell Stone
in 1938, continues to the symbol of and
entrance to the Museum and maintains
its historic relationship with the rest
of the block.

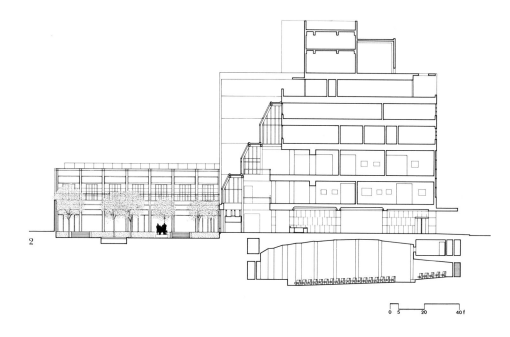

1

2

0 5   20   40 f

1 Night view into sculpture garden
2 Section looking east
3 View of Garden Hall
4 Gallery view
5 View of expansion and residential tower

3

4

5

Four Leaf/Four Oaks Towers

Design/Completion 1979/1982
Houston, Texas
Interfin Corporation
1,000,000 square feet (Four Leaf)
1,720,000 square feet (Four Oaks)
Flat slab, reinforced concrete structural system
Four Leaf: tinted vision glass curtain wall with three colors of ceramic glass
Four Oaks: grey reflective vision glass curtain wall with two shades of blue opaque ceramic glass

Four Leaf Towers, twin 40-story residences, are topped with truncated, pyramidal roofs. The rich colors of the facade are interwoven to create a shiny, textural pattern. The 9.5- acre site includes a swimming pool, tennis courts, gymnasium, saunas, landscaped gardens and below-grade parking.

Four Oaks Towers consists of four office buildings: two 25-story towers, a central 30-story tower and a 12-story headquarters for Interfin Corporation. They are the terminus of the north view of Post Oak Boulevard. A ground-level arcade links the towers and provides access to the garage.

1

1   View of Four Leaf Towers
2   View of Four Leaf/Four Oaks Towers
3   Four Leaf Towers site plan
4   Four Oaks Towers site plan

2

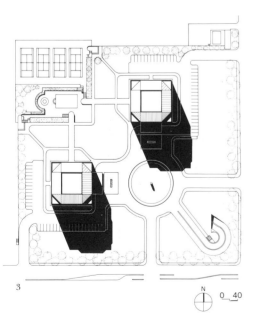

3

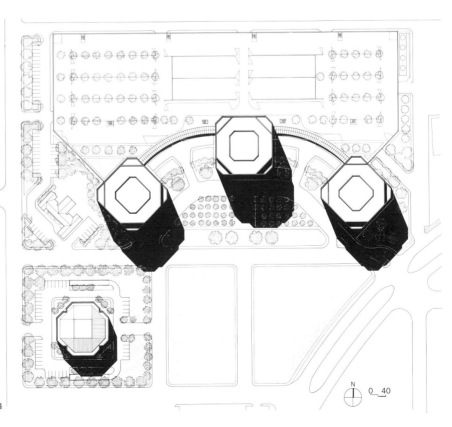

4

N   0 40

N   0 40

Pacific Design Center (Phase I), Pacific Design Center Expansion (Phases II and III)

Design/Completion 1971/1975; 1984/1988
West Hollywood, California
Sequoia Pacific, a division of Southern Pacific Company
Phase I: 750,000 square feet
Phase II: 470,000 square feet
Steel structural frame
Phase I: opaque blue ceramic glass
Phase II: opaque green ceramic glass
Phase III (future): opaque red ceramic glass

The Pacific Design Center (PDC) provides showroom space for interior designers and others involved in contract and residential design.

PDC I built in 1975, was conceived as a single free-standing structure. The decision to expand the Center raised the complex issue of how to add to a distinctive landmark. The original was an isolated form; phases II and III were designed as a series of oversized fragments forming a collection of pieces. Each has a unique shape and color, although using the same materials, scale and detailing.

Phase II built in 1988, includes showrooms, parking, a conference center with a 450–seat auditorium and a public plaza with an outdoor amphitheater and a 5,000 square-foot exhibition gallery.

PDC III is planned to accommodate future growth.

1

1   View north from West Hollywood
    toward Phases I and II
2   Site plan
3–8 Study models (Phases I, II and III)

2

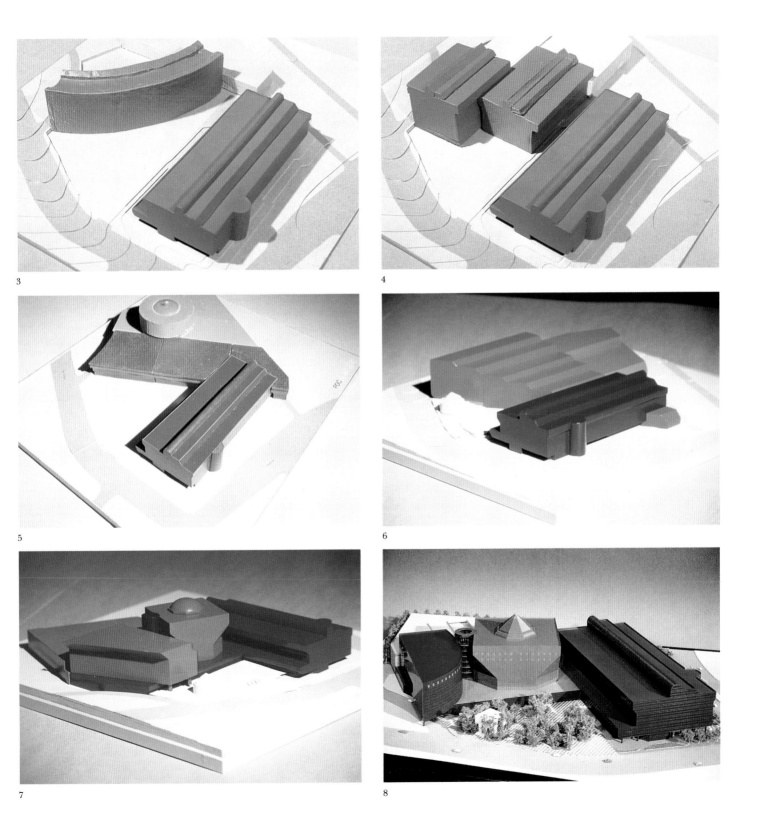

3

4

5

6

7

8

10

11

9 View toward junction from Phase I and Phase II
   with garage
10 View of ceiling skylight from interior
11 View from inside circulation cylinder
12 Night view of circulation cylinder
13 West elevation

12

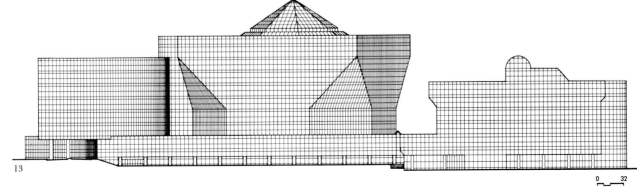

13

0 ___ 32

St Luke's Medical Tower

Design/Completion 1987/1990
Houston, Texas
St Luke's Episcopal Hospital
and Hines Interests Limited Partnership
485,000 square feet with garage parking for 1,350 cars
Precast and cast-in-place concrete
Reflective vision and spandrel glass, white-metal mullions,
cornice rail and spires

The 25-story St Luke's Medical Tower
is a state-of-the-art medical facility
and teaching hospital, straddling a block
between two major streets, Fannin and
Main. Designed in response to this dual
frontage, the twin octagonal towers help
to define the urban environment. From
all vantage points, St Luke's is a significant
addition to the Houston skyline—an
optimistic and uplifting structure.

1

1 Perspective sketches
2 Typical tower floor plan
3 Site plan
4 Street-level plan
5 View of tower from Fannin Street

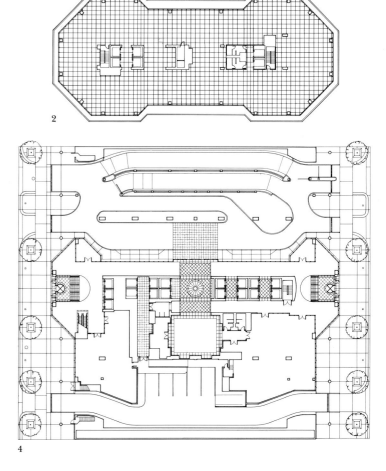

2

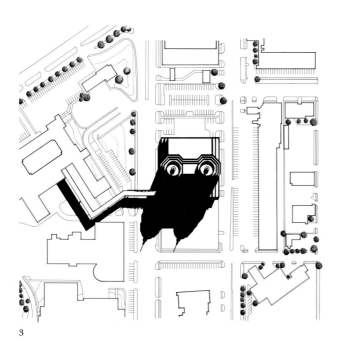

3

4

38

5

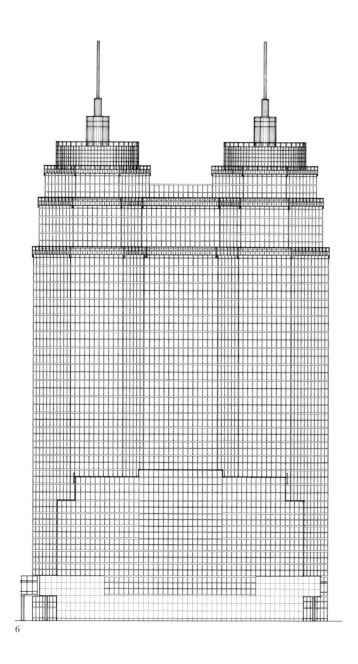

6

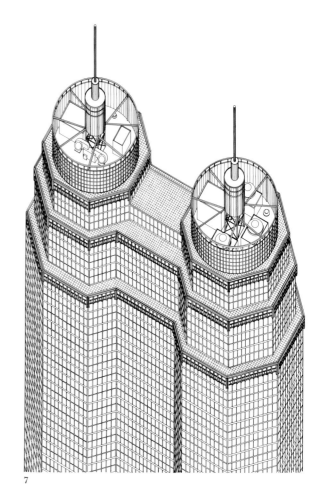

7

8

6 Elevation
7 Axonometric of building top
8 View of skybridge from Fannin Street
9 Night view of tower

9

Stone

US Embassy, Tokyo

Design/Completion 1972/1975
Tokyo, Japan
United States Department of State
245,000 square feet
Reinforced concrete frame
Scored cast-stone panels and operable
awning windows

The US Embassy in Tokyo is one of the
three largest American embassies.
The 11-story tower and three-story wing
are separated by two courtyards, gardens,
terraces and an auditorium.

The exterior wall is a modular grid that
corresponds with the modular plan of the
interior office space. The structure is made
visible at the end of the building and
at ground level, where it forms an entrance
portico. Designed to meet earthquake
safety codes of both Tokyo and California,
the building also responds to both
American and Japanese aesthetic tradition.

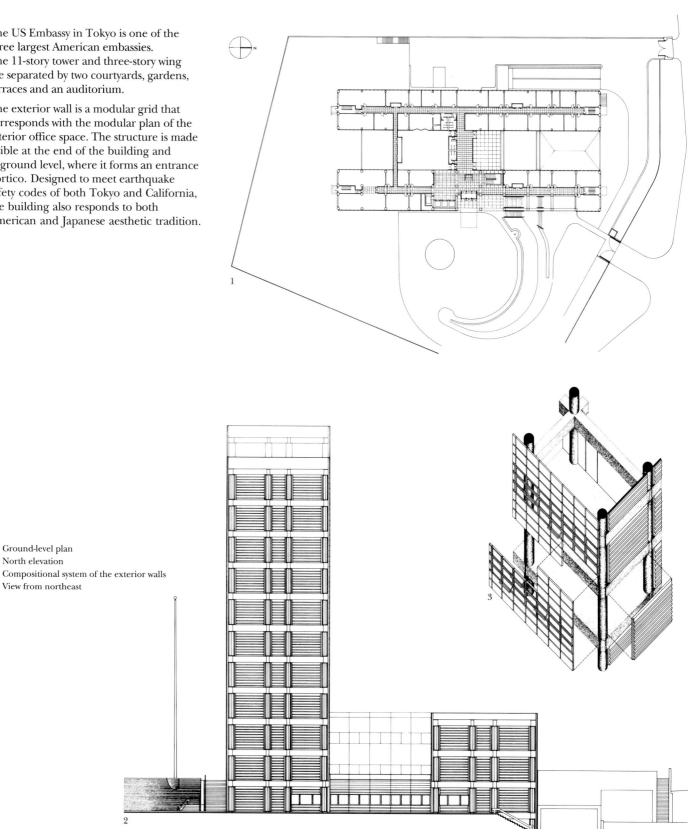

1   Ground-level plan
2   North elevation
3   Compositional system of the exterior walls
4   View from northeast

4

Crile Clinic Building

Design/Completion 1980/1984
Cleveland, Ohio
Cleveland Clinic Foundation
620,000 square feet
Reinforced concrete frame
Granite and glass

The Crile Building and the Cleveland Clinic Green represent the first phase in the development of the Cleveland Clinic Foundation's Master Plan for a medical campus.

The two-acre Cleveland Clinic Green is a central open space and unifying core around which future buildings can be developed. The Crile Building accommodates 21 clinics, ranging in size from 4,500 to 55,000 square feet. Each two-floor complex acts as a separate unit, unified by the nature of its medical services and by a two-story atrium.

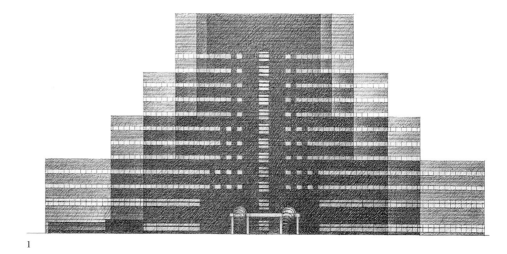

1

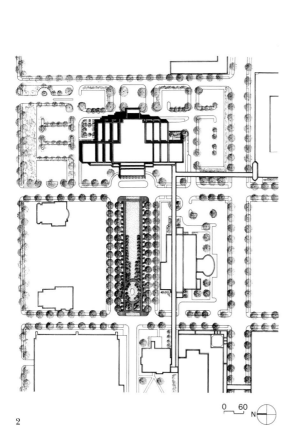

2

0 60 N

3

4

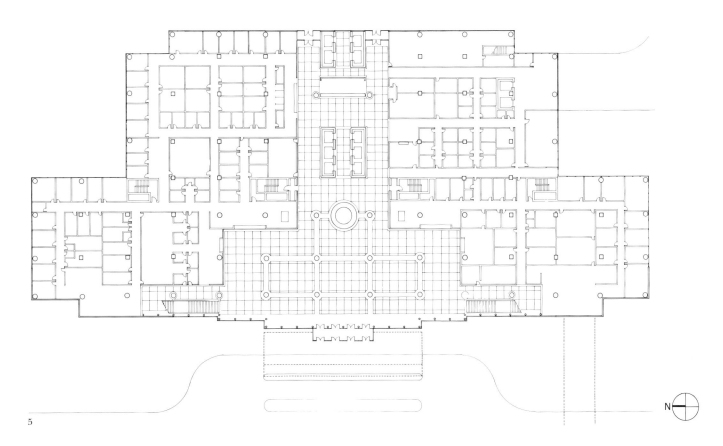

5

1   Rendering of elevation
2   Site plan
3   View of building from Cleveland Clinic Green
4   West elevation
5   Ground-level plan

Norwest Center/Gaviidae Common

Design/Completion 1985/1989 (Norwest); 1986/1989 (Gaviidae)
Minneapolis, Minnesota
Hines Interests Limited Partnership (Norwest)
BCE Development Properties Inc. (Gaviidae)
1,300,000 square feet (Norwest); 315,000 square feet (Gaviidae)
Steel tube complemented by four concrete super columns (Norwest)
Amber Minnesota stone and thin vertical bands of white marble (Norwest)
Beige French limestone with green slate (Gaviidae)

Norwest Center was designed to capture the spirit of the city in its architecture. Multiple steps give it a distinctive silhouette and relate it to pedestrian scale. The skybridge across Marquette Avenue, designed by Cesar Pelli in collaboration with public artist Siah Armajani, is filled with color and light, becoming a celebratory arch for traffic below and a marker for pedestrian movement above.

Gaviidae Common adjoins Norwest Center, further integrating it with the downtown area. A second skybridge, also designed in collaboration with Armajani, connects Gaviidae with City Center. Gaviidae comprises five levels of retail and below-grade parking. The dramatic five-story atrium is covered by a barrel vault finished with a blue geometrical stencilled pattern with gold-leaf accents.

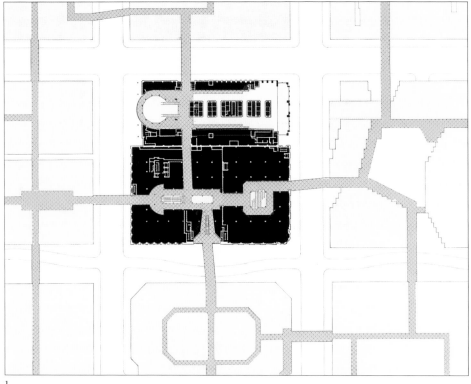

1

2

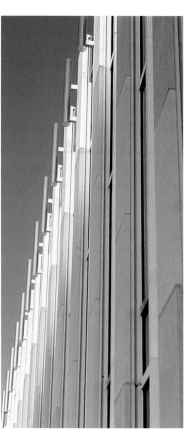

3

1 Second-floor plan with skyway system
2 General view, looking south
3 Setback accent detail
4 General view showing context

4

5 Entrance detail
6 View of rotunda from street level
7 Worm's-eye axonometric section of rotunda
8 First-floor plan
9 View of rotunda interior

5

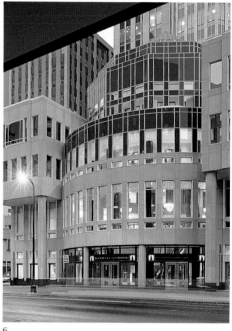

6

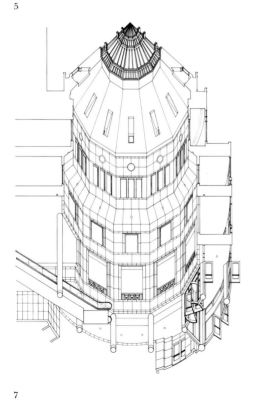

7

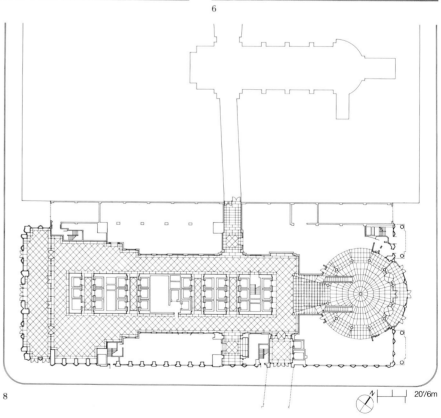

8

20'/6m

9

10 View southwest down Marquette Avenue
11 Skybridge across Marquette Avenue
12 Connection of skybridge to Gaviidae Common
    along Nicollet Mall
13 Gaviidae concourse interior

11

10

12

13

World Financial Center and Winter Garden

Design/Completion 1980/1988
New York, New York
Olympia & York Equity Corporation
8,600,000 square feet
Steel frame
Sagami and carnelian granite; reflective,
clear and ceramic glass; copper roofs

The World Financial Center creates major
public forms that continue and celebrate
the historic skyline of Manhattan. It consists
of four office towers ranging in height from
34 to 51 stories, the public Winter Garden,
a glass-roofed courtyard, two 9-story
octagonal gateway buildings and
a 3.5-acre landscaped public plaza.

The proportion of granite to glass is greater
at the base of each tower and gradually
lightens into a completely reflective glass
skin. At various intervals the towers are set
back and ascend to distinctively shaped
copper tops.

The skyscrapers surround and define
a public plaza at the waterfront. Adjacent
to the plaza, the Winter Garden creates
a great public room enclosed in a glass
vault 125 feet high. Lined with shops and
restaurants, the Winter Garden acts as the
project's and the city's living room.
It is a great everyday meeting place
and a place for extraordinary events.

1

1   Night view from across the Hudson River
2   View east from across the Hudson River
3   Axonometric

2

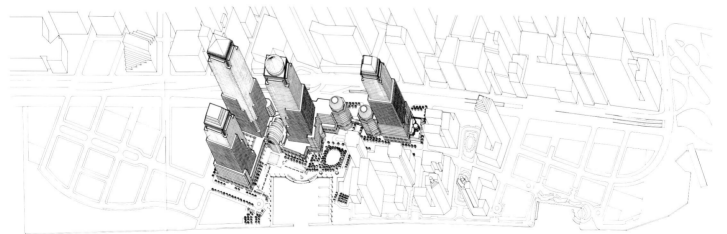

3

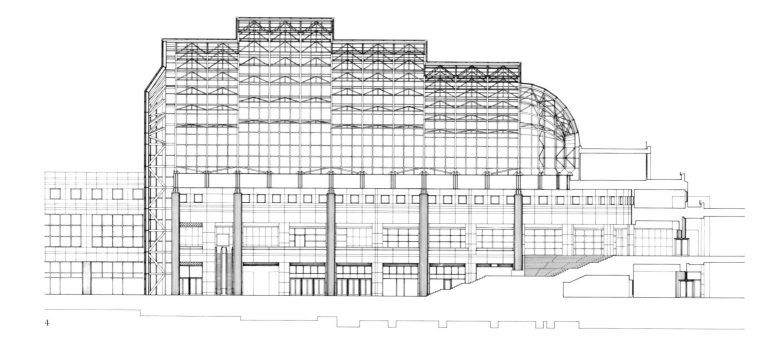

4

5

6

4 Winter Garden section, view north
5 Night view east of Winter Garden
6 Interior view of structural vault
7 Winter Garden interior, view east

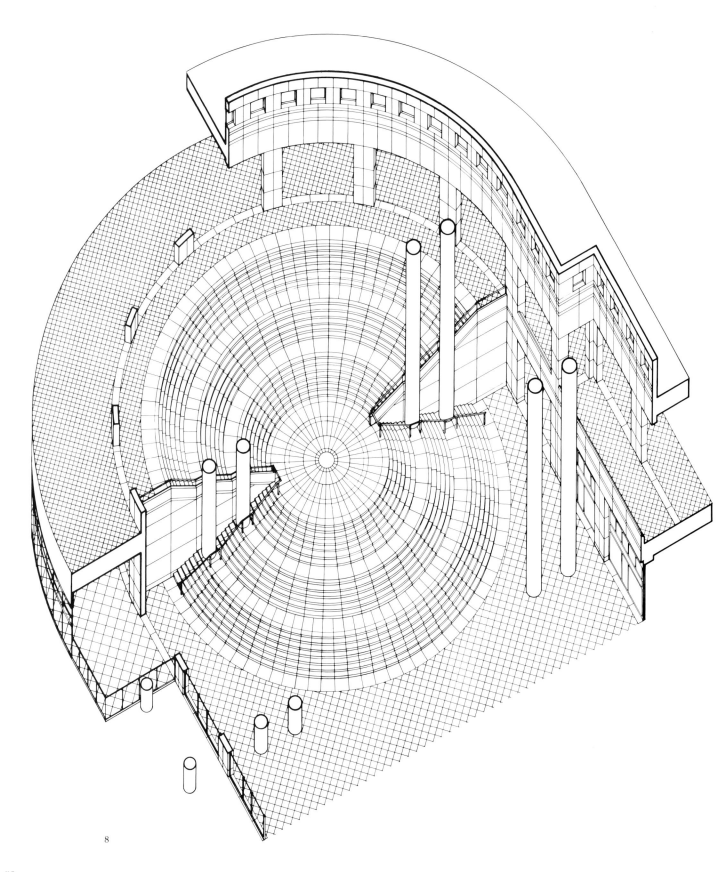

8

8 Cutaway axonometric of monumental stair
   in Winter Garden
9 Winter Garden interior, view west

9

10 Winter Garden stairway detail
11 Interior of Winter Garden
12 Night view of performance inside Winter Garden
13 Interior of Winter Garden
14 Event inside Winter Garden

10

11

12

13

14

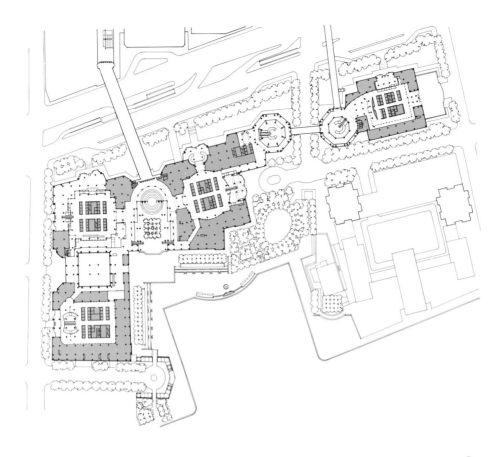

15

16

15 Second-floor level of public and circulation space
16 Ground-floor level of public and circulation space
17 Plaza, view north
18 View north over plaza

17

18

NationsBank Corporate Center and Founders Hall

Design/Completion 1987/1992
Charlotte, North Carolina
NationsBank Corporation, Charter Properties and Lincoln Property Company
1,200,000 square feet
Poured-in-place concrete
Vermont green marble, thermal agate and Texas sunset rose granite;
top created by aluminum masts

The NationsBank Corporate Center is in the historic, geographic and business center of Charlotte. The Center includes the 60-story NationsBank corporate headquarters tower, a landscaped plaza and Founders Hall— a large public room.

Founders Hall is a grand civic space directly connected to the North Carolina Blumenthal Performing Arts Center and the Overstreet Mall. It unifies the site, providing an entry hall to NationsBank Tower. A circular monumental stair accommodates a natural stage. It is the meeting place for Charloteens and the hall for public events.

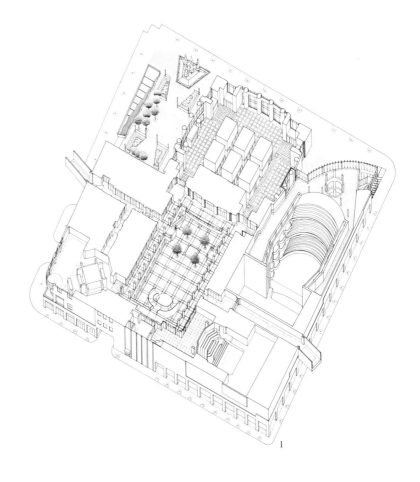

1

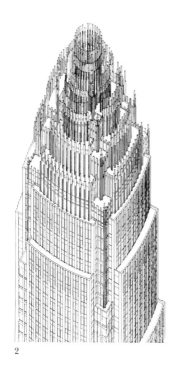

2

3

1 Ground-level axonometric
2 Tower top axonometric
3 Tower top
4 General view of tower

4

5

6

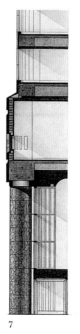

7

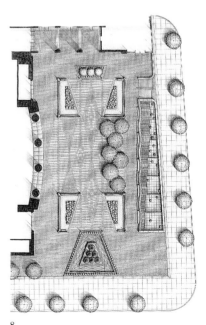

8

5 View of plaza and tower entrance
6–8 Renderings of base elevation, base section
and plaza plan
9 View of lobby interior
10 View of elevators
11 General view of lobby

9

10

11

12 Night view of tower and Founders Hall
13 View north of Founders Hall
14 Lateral section of Founders Hall

12

13

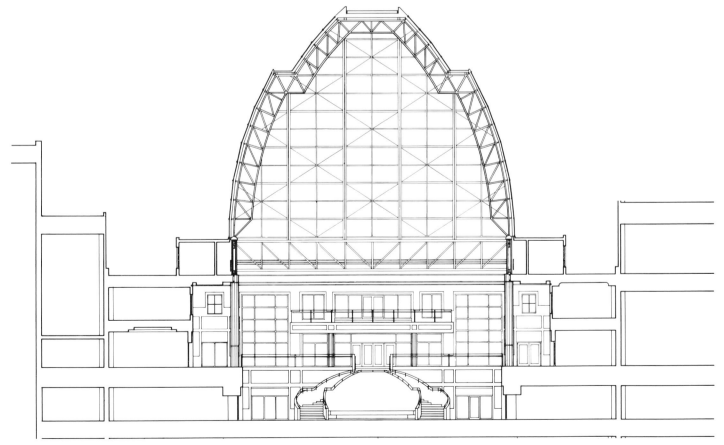

14

15 Interior view of Founders Hall
16 Skywalk level of Founders Hall

15

Society Center

Design/Completion 1987/1992
Cleveland, Ohio
Richard & David Jacobs Group
1,250,000 square feet
Composite steel and concrete
Stony Creek granite, stainless steel
trim, stainless steel top

On a corner site, Society Center faces both
the Public Square and the Mall, defining
and linking Cleveland's two most important
historic downtown public places.
In combination with the Terminal and BP
America Towers, the new 57-story tower
locates Public Square on Cleveland's skyline
and creates a landmark silhouette for the
center of Cleveland.

The design of Society Center also included
rehabilitation of the historic Society for
Savings Bank (designed by Burnham and
Root in 1889), and a 403-room convention
hotel which completes the full-block
development known as Society Center.

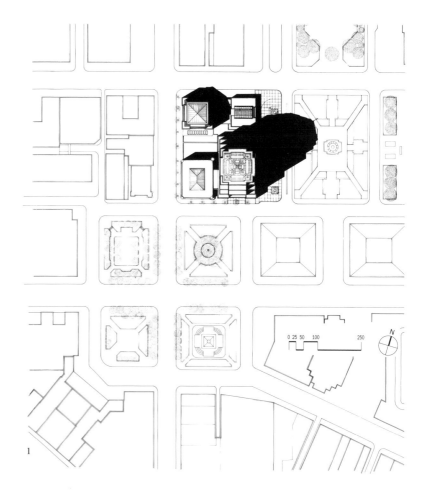

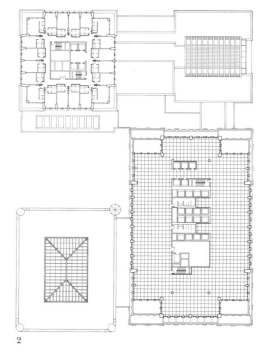

1   Site plan
2   Typical low to mid-rise floor plan
3   General view of tower, bank and hotel

3

4

5

6

7

8

Yerba Buena Tower

Design/Completion 1988/
San Francisco, California
Olympia & York Equity Corporation and California Equities
786,000 square feet
Steel frame
Light beige French limestone,
clear glass top, rolled steel sculptural forms

Considerable attention was paid
to designing a building sympathetic with
San Francisco, a city of well-defined
architectural character, scale and color.
The sculptural top was a collaboration
between public artist Siah Armajani and
Cesar Pelli. It is a grand celebratory gesture
in the best tradition of the city.

The collaboration between Pelli and
Armajani stretches the natural boundaries
of architecture and public art. It sought
to integrate the building top, shaft and
functional requirements. The top, rising
127 feet above the tower, is a complex
assemblage of rolled steel sections
accommodating mechanical, electrical
and elevator equipment.

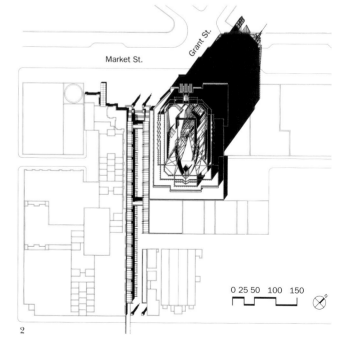

1

1 Photographic montage, view northwest
2 Site plan
3 Tower top
4 West elevation
5 Tower top
6 Tower top

2

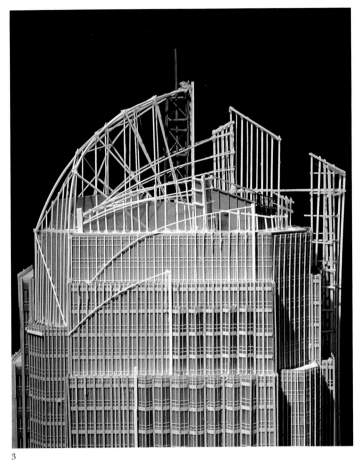

3

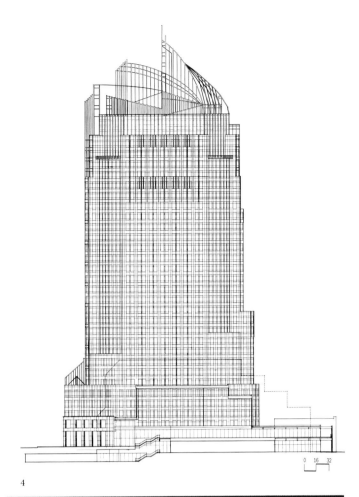

4

5

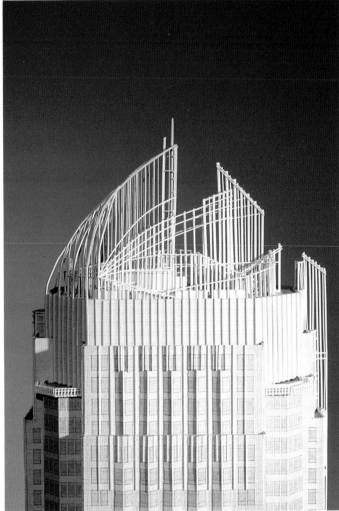

6

181 West Madison

Design/Completion 1986/1990
Chicago, Illinois
Miglin-Beitler Developments
1,000,000 square feet
Composite structure: center-braced reinforced concrete core with a perimeter
of steel columns (semi or soft tube structure, columns 20 feet on center)
Granite-clad piers with glass infill; stainless steel fins at roof edge

181 West Madison is a 50-story tower,
organized with a square floor plan and
column-free office space in a five-foot
regular module. The exterior wall expresses
this five-foot module with vertical
granite ribs.

At its base, a four-story glass-roofed loggia
at Madison Street serves as a transitional
element to the building lobby. Clad in warm
white, gray and green marbles, the lobby's
tall main hall has a vaulted coffered ceiling.
A large glass wall along Madison Street
floods the lobby with natural light.

1   Rendering of north elevation
2   Site plan
3   Ground-floor plan
4   View of entrance loggia

1

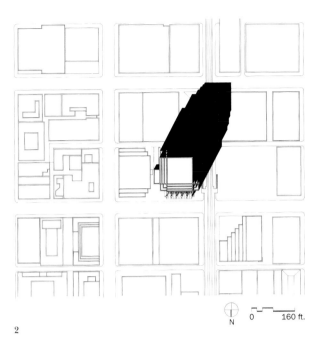

2

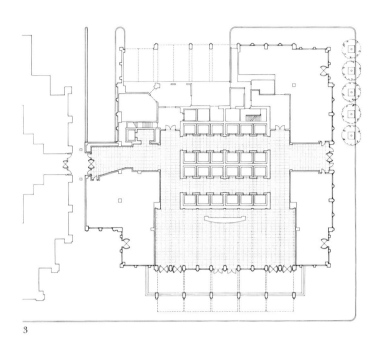

3

4

5

6

5–8 Views of lobby, elevator lobby and elevator
9 North elevation

7

8

9

Miglin-Beitler Tower

Design/Completion 1988/
Chicago, Illinois
Miglin-Beitler Developments
1,900,000 square feet
Cruciform tube form; concrete piers
Granite, stainless steel

The Miglin-Beitler Tower will rise 125
stories and measure 2,000 feet from
its base to the top of the spire.
Because of the structural demands
on a building of this height, structure
and architecture are one. Two massive
concrete piers on each side of the building
align with the interior core, enabling
essentially column-free interior spaces.
With setbacks reading along the height
of the building, the piers reinforce the
upward motion of the tower, adding
visual as well as structural solidity.

1   General view of study model
2   Elevation
3   View of study model tower top
4   Typical floor plan

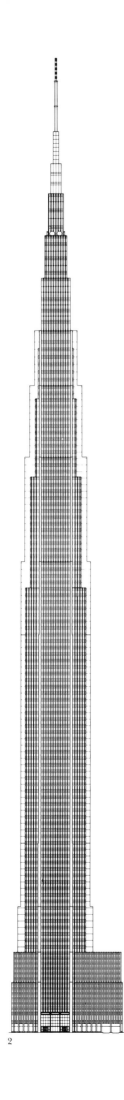

2

3

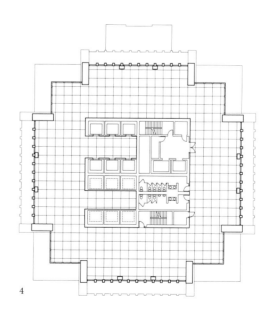

4

Metal

COMSAT Laboratories

Design/Completion 1967/1969
Clarksburg, Maryland
Communications Satellite Corporation
245,000 square feet
Steel
Clear anodized aluminum panels

The building is located on a 210-acre
site in the Maryland countryside.
Core and support laboratories, research
and administrative offices, spacecraft
assembly and related public spaces provide
functions necessary to research, develop
and produce communications satellites.

The plan gathers spaces off a central spine.
The spine serves as the common room or
meeting place, connecting the laboratories
and enclosing the courtyards.

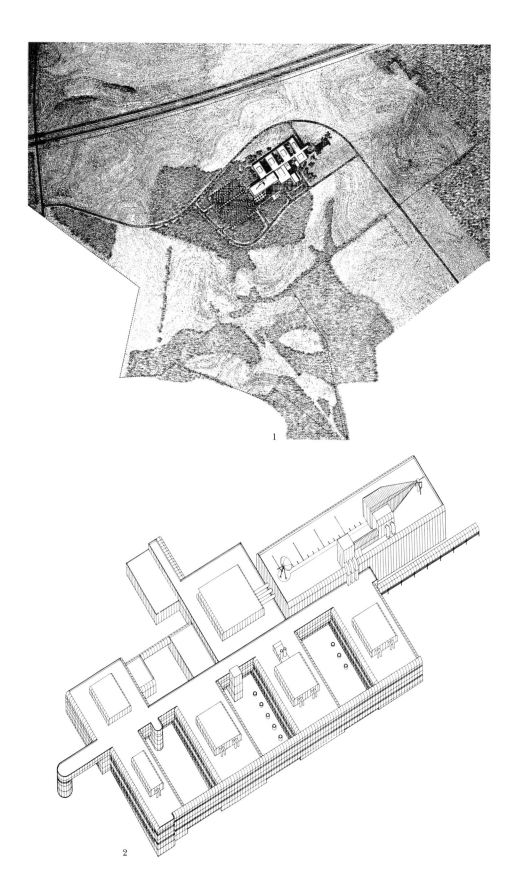

1

2

1 Site plan
2 Axonometric
3 General night view
4 First-floor plan
5–7 Diagrams showing: predetermined growth,
   corridor and spaces; views

3

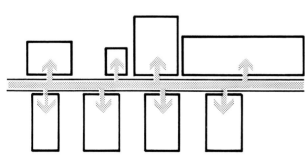

4

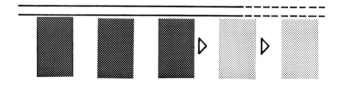

5   Predetermined growth

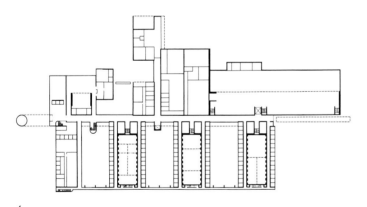

Corridor and spaces

6

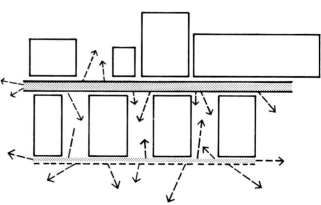

7   Views

Canary Wharf Tower, Retail and Assembly Building and Docklands Light Railway Station

Design/Completion 1987/1991
Docklands, London, England
Olympia & York Canary Wharf Ltd
1,800,000 square feet
Steel frame, concrete (Assembly Building)
Stainless steel, glass, limestone (Assembly Building)

Considered England's first skyscraper, the 48-story tower is a landmark for the entire Canary Wharf complex. A tall, square prism with indented corners that culminate in a square pyramid against the sky, the building is completely clad in stainless steel.

The Retail and Assembly Building is a 250,000 square-foot structure that includes shops and restaurants, as well as the central Assembly Hall with adjoining meeting and exhibition rooms. The Assembly Hall supports musical and dramatic performances, trade shows and meetings.

The Docklands Light Railway Station is located at the second floor level, connected to the tower through the concourse. Its roof is a glass and steel vault spanning 120 feet— a modern reinterpretation of the great vaulted spaces of London's 19th century railway stations.

1

1 Rendering of Tower, view east
2 View of Tower from Greenwich
3 General view of Tower from city

2

3

4 South elevation
5 Ground-level plan
6 Section through Docklands Light Railway Station
7 Roof plan of Tower, Retail and Assembly Building,
  and Docklands Light Railway Station

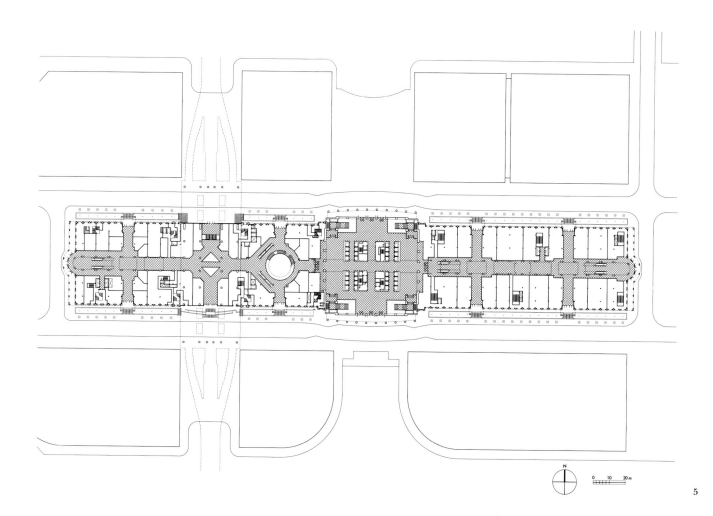

4

5

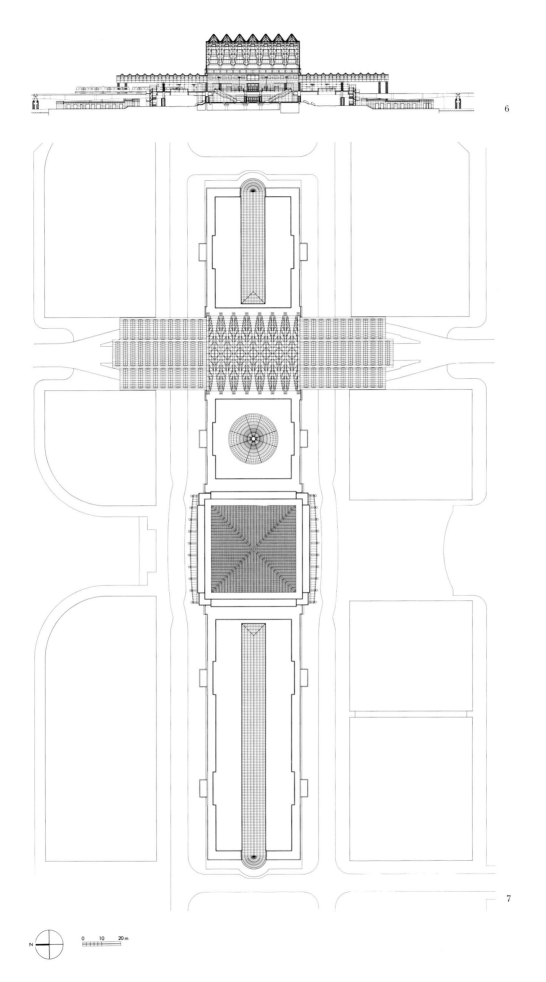

6

7

N

0 10 20 m

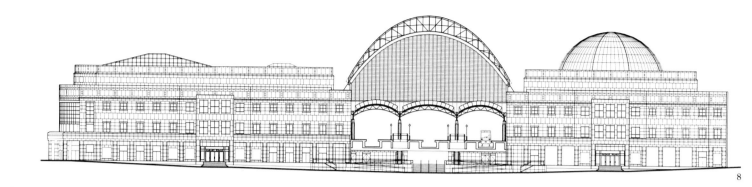

8

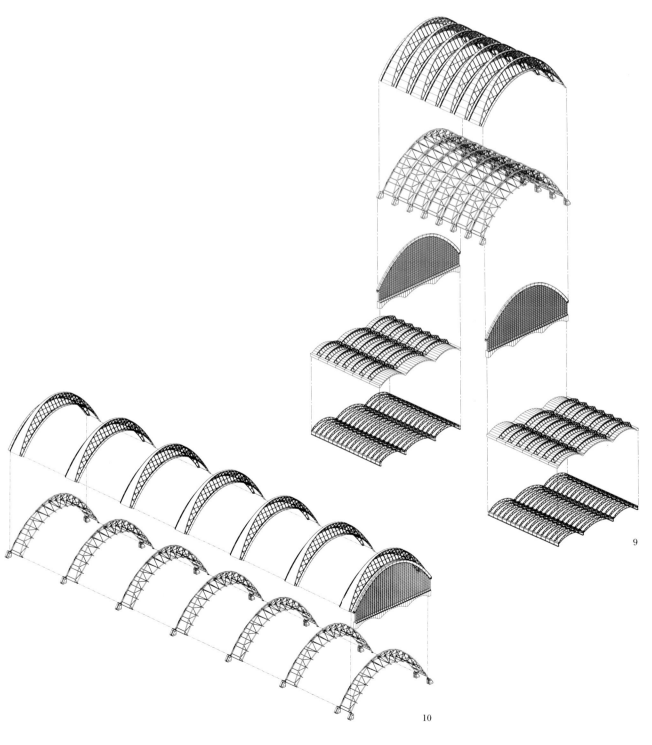

9

10

11

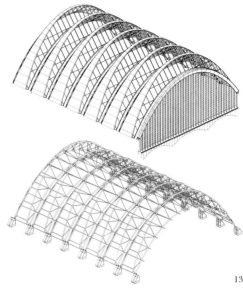

13

8 South elevation of Retail and Assembly Building and Docklands Light Railway Station
9 Docklands Light Railway Station exploded roof axonometric
10 Docklands Light Railway Station exploded vault structure axonometric and skylights
11 Night view of Docklands Light Railway Station
12 View of construction of Docklands Light Railway Station
13 Roof vaults with skylights

12

777 Tower

Design/Completion 1987/1990
Los Angeles, California
South Figueroa Plaza Associates
1,100,000 square feet
Structural steel (perimeter tube)
Curved fluoropolymer-painted aluminum panels

Rising 53 stories, 777 Tower is visible from
the Santa Monica and Harbor freeways.
Bowed on the east and west sides, the tower
has three setbacks, each articulated with
flared accents to enhance its silhouette.
Deeply sculptured forms capture the
southern California light and generate
shadows and highlights along the shaft.

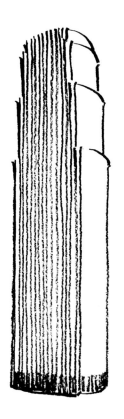

1

L.A. TOWER, C. PELLI, 88

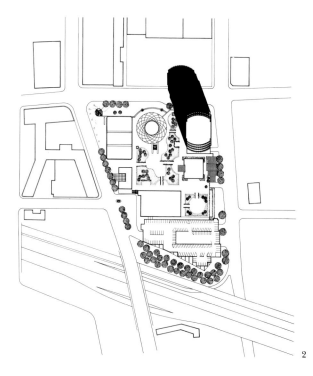

2

1   Sketch by Cesar Pelli
2   Site plan
3   View of curtain wall, showing flared,
    painted aluminum accents

3

4

5

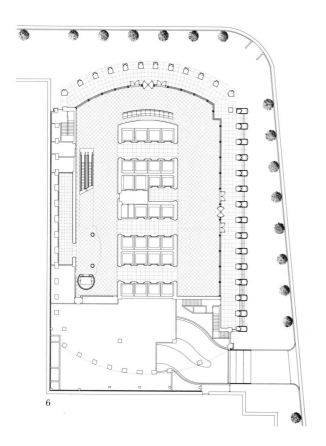

6

7

4   View of lobby entrance
5   View of aluminum-clad arcade
6   Ground-level plan
7   View of lobby
8   General view of Tower

8

Plaza Tower

Design/Completion 1989/1991
Costa Mesa, California
C.J. Segerstrom & Sons Inc.
480,000 square feet
Steel frame
Stainless steel panels

1   General view of Tower
2   View of Tower base
3   Tower curtain wall

Rising 21 stories, Plaza Tower is the newest member of the family of buildings of South Coast Plaza Town Center.

Stainless steel, a material that connotes strength, durability and precision, is also a material of great visual and sensual richness. Form and materials are well integrated in the design of Plaza Tower. A double grid of vertical and horizontal ribs give the exterior wall scale and texture. The rounded edges of the ribs catch the light, tracing highlights on the wall.

1

2

4

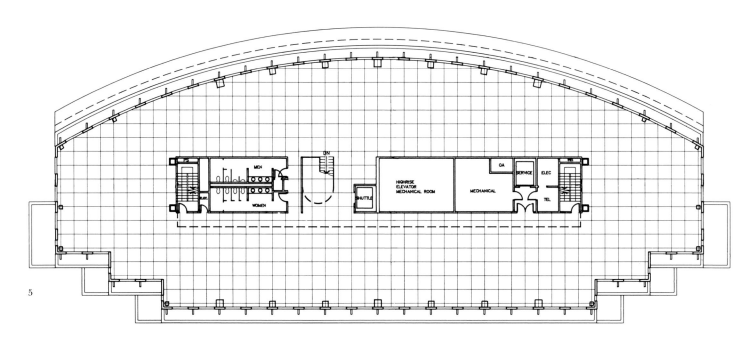

5

6

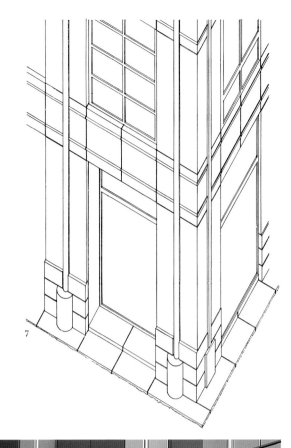

7

8

NTT Shinjuku Headquarters Building

Design/Completion 1990/1995
Tokyo, Japan
NTT Corporation
645,000 square feet
Tower: Concrete-encased steel structure
Special Purpose Building: Poured-in-place concrete
Tower: Fluoropolymer-coated aluminum panels with metallic gray finish
Special Purpose Building: Minnesota Stone, green Vermont slate

The NTT Shinjuku Headquarters Building
is a 30-story tower, including corporate
offices and a 6-level below-grade
telecommunications center. Attached
to the tower is a 45,000 square foot special
purpose building with three floors
of exhibition space and a 150-seat
below-grade auditorium. The tower
and special purpose building are linked
at mezzanine level by a pedestrian bridge
overlooking an open garden.

The project is an extension of the cultural,
corporate and commercial center
of Shinjuku, six blocks from the new
Tokyo City Hall and across the street from
Opera House City. The triangular tower
responds to sunshine access regulations—
no single point of neighboring residential
properties are under shadow for more than
three hours each day. The building also
responds to site limitations (including
an elevated highway), open space
requirements, two existing microwave
corridors and accommodation
of a helicopter landing area.

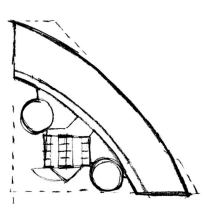

2

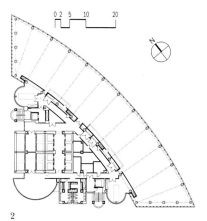

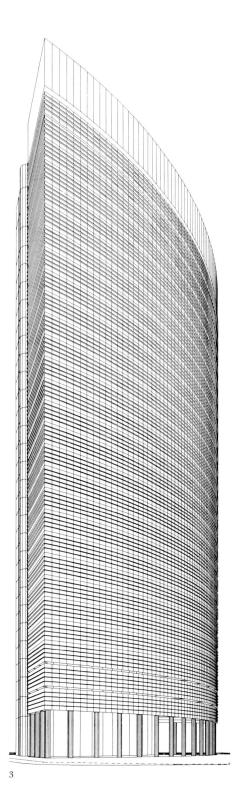

1

3

1 Sketch by Cesar Pelli
2 Typical lower floor plan
3 Computer generated perspective view
of tower
4 South elevation of model

4

5

5   Model, view from southeast corner
6   Site plan
7   Diagram showing three-hour shadow restriction
8   Diagram showing best views

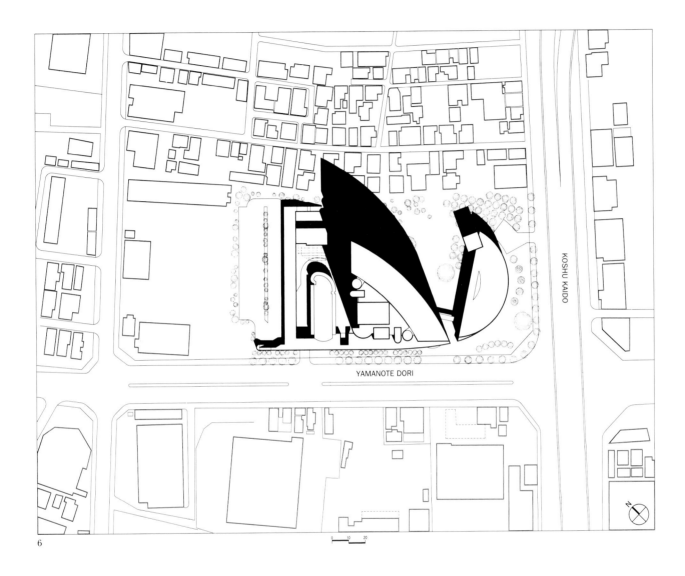

6

KOSHU KAIDO

YAMANOTE DORI

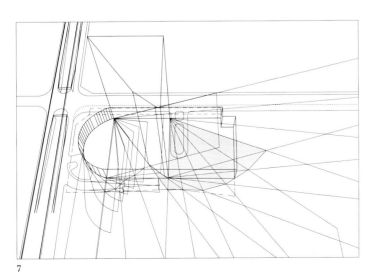

7

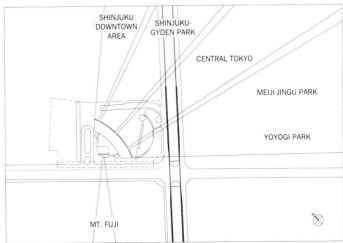

SHINJUKU
DOWNTOWN
AREA

SHINJUKU-
GYDEN PARK

CENTRAL TOKYO

MEIJI-JINGU PARK

YOYOGI PARK

MT. FUJI

8

9

9　View of plaza and special purpose building
10　Computer generated perspective view of special purpose building
11　Landscape plan of plaza
12　Axonometric of fence

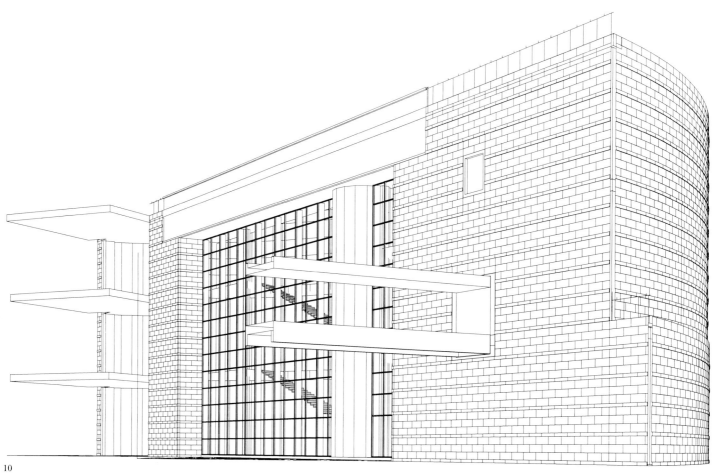

10

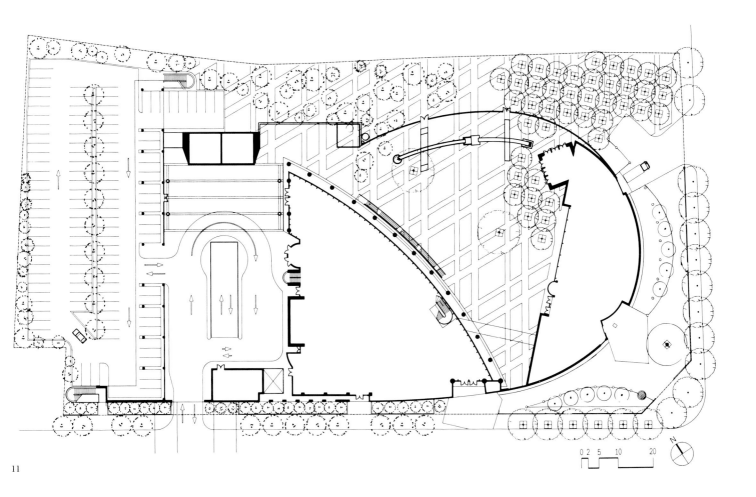

11

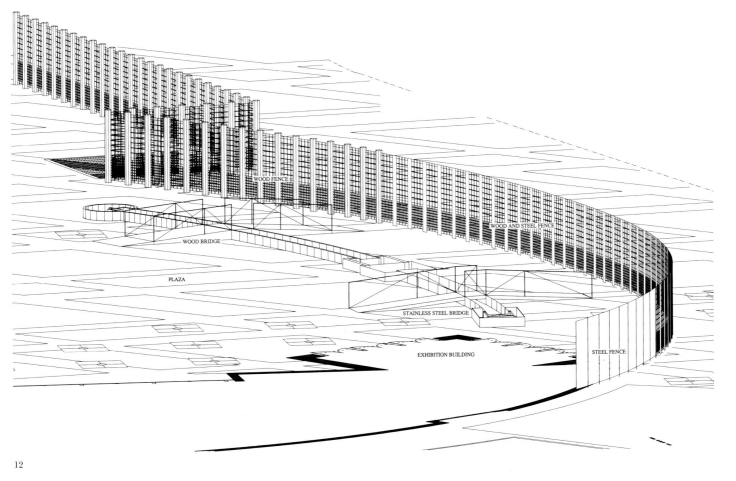

WOOD FENCE

WOOD AND STEEL FENCE

WOOD BRIDGE

PLAZA

STAINLESS STEEL BRIDGE

EXHIBITION BUILDING

STEEL FENCE

12

New North Terminal, Washington National Airport

Design/Completion 1990/1996
Washington, DC
Metropolitan Washington Airports Authority
1,000,000 square feet
Steel columns, vaulted roof-dome trusses
Clear, patterned and spandrel glass with painted aluminum mullion
system; painted metal panels and louvers; precast concrete

The Washington National Airport is situated on a landfill site on the southwest side of the Potomac River, in direct view of the Federal Core and the Mall. The terminal is located between the historic South Terminal and hangars at the north end of the airport. With 35 gates, the three-level terminal includes a 1,200-foot concourse designed to accommodate 16 million passengers per year. Its cross-section provides direct connection with the Metro station and maximizes views of the airfield and Federal Core. The design is based on a repetitive 45 foot square structural steel bay that establishes scale, flexibility and architectural proportions. Two new parking garages are being designed concurrently with the terminal.

1

2

1   Site model, view south
2   Site model, view north
3   Washington, DC context
4   Site plan
5   Night rendering of ticketing level

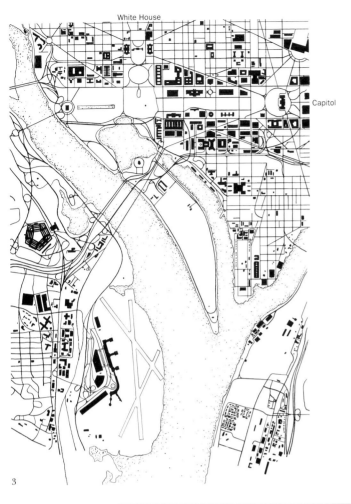

White House

Capitol

3

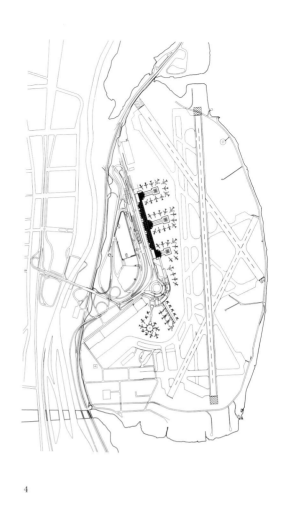

4

5

6   Ticketing-level plan
7   Concourse-level plan
8   Baggage-level plan
9   Night rendering of apron view
10 (Inset) Night view (ca 1950) of 1941 South Terminal

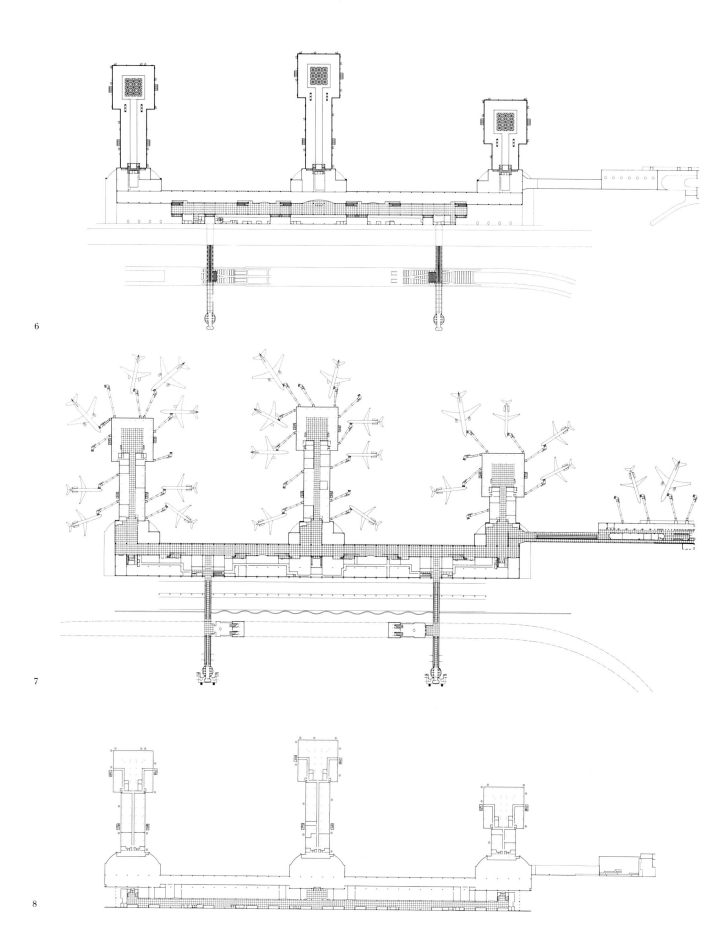

6

7

8

9

10

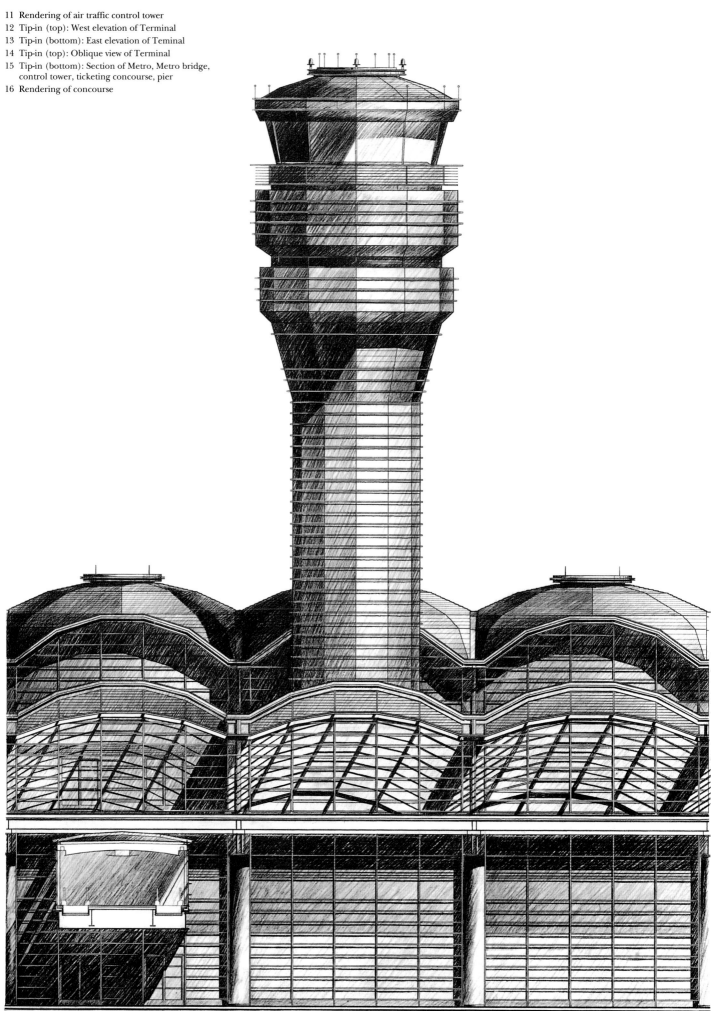

11

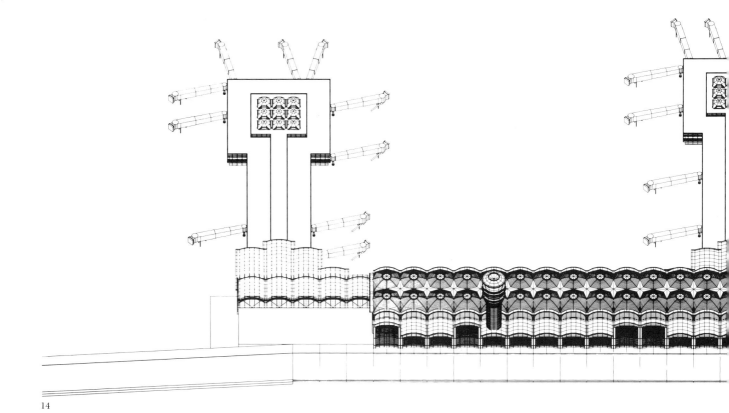

14

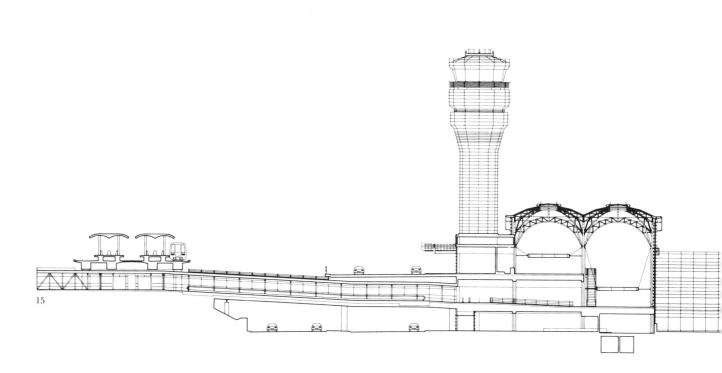

15

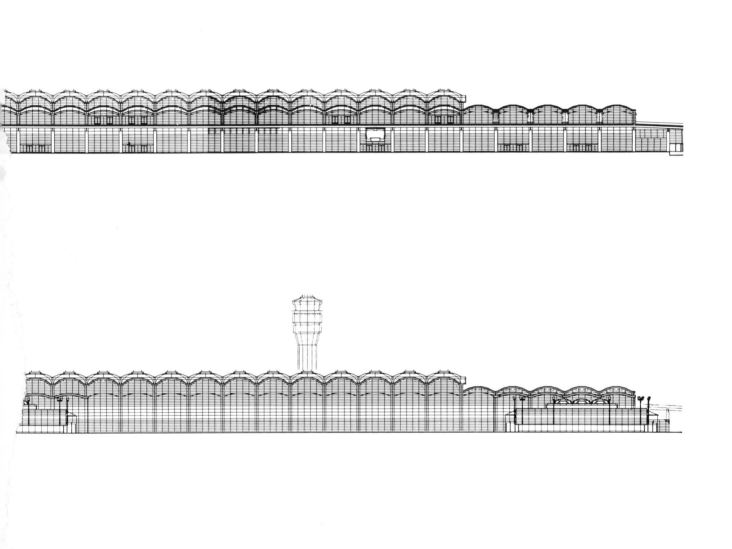

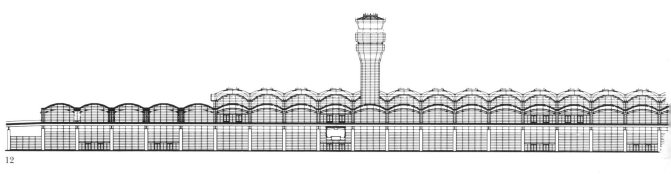

12

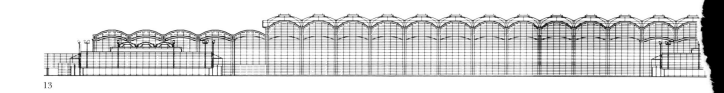

13

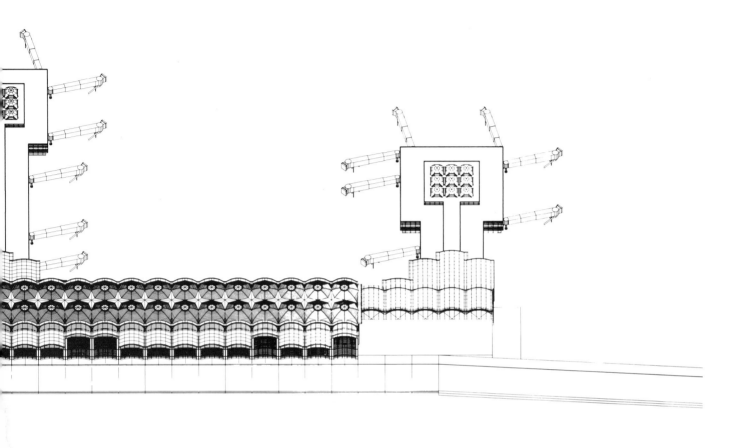
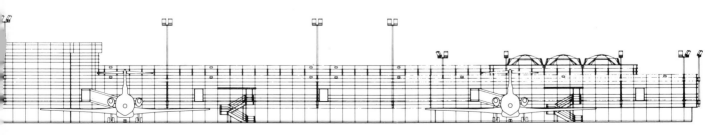

16

18

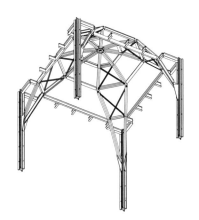

17

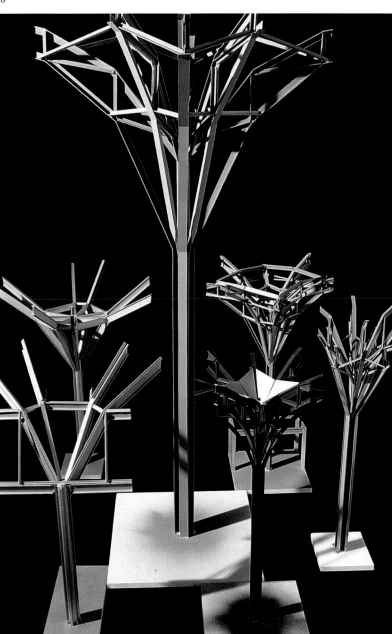

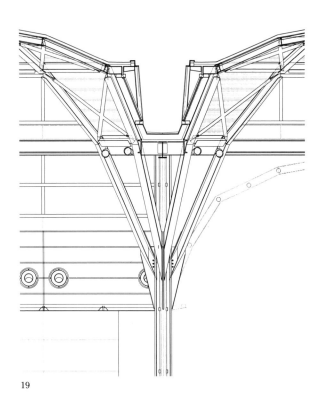

19

20

21

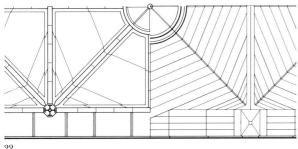

22

23

24

25

17   Pier dome axonometric details (three details)
18   Dome study models
19   Pier dome sectional detail
20   Dome column study models
21   Exploded axonometric of domes
22   Reflected ceiling plan, roof plan
23   Model view of main concourse
         and ticketing concourse
24–25 Curtain-wall models

26   Studio
27   Early study models of four alternatives
28–33   Study models of alternative schemes

26

27

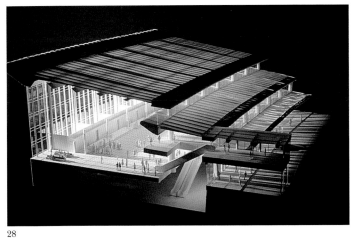

28

29

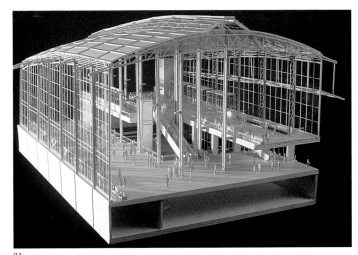

30

31

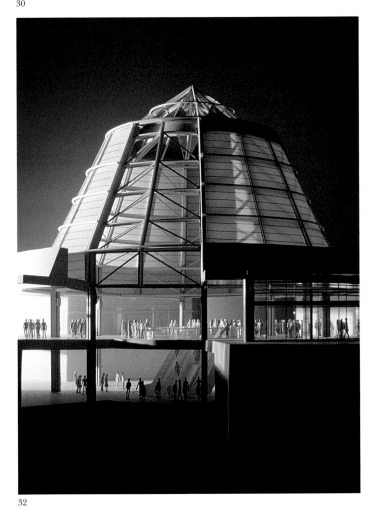

32

33

One Market

Design/Completion 1991/1994
San Francisco, California
Yarmouth Group
1,500,000 square feet
Steel
Aluminum, stainless steel, marble

One Market is a multi-tenant office building complex located in the San Francisco central business district. The existing complex, built in the 1970s, includes two office towers, public spaces and retailing. Cesar Pelli & Associates designed major improvements to public and retail spaces throughout the project.

Interior and exterior spaces were transformed, creating a new destination point for the city. A 131-foot high lattice pavilion redefines a centrally located courtyard. A gate tower that echoes the forms of the lattice pavilion stands in the Mission Street plaza, marking not only a major entrance to One Market, but also the bayside edge of the city. Expanded lobbies for each office tower are enriched and redefined with patterned marble floors and walls, and vaulted ceilings.

1

1   Study rendering of plaza and gate tower
2   Axonometric of renovation

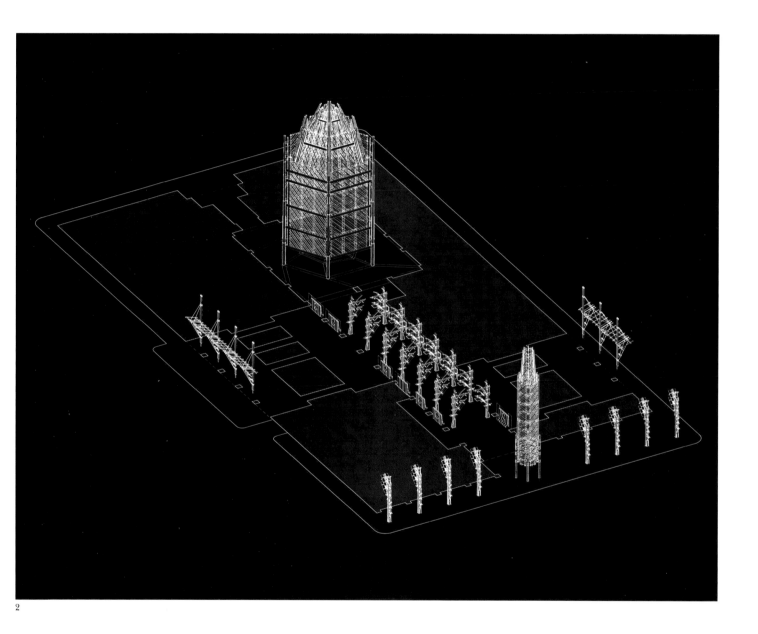

2

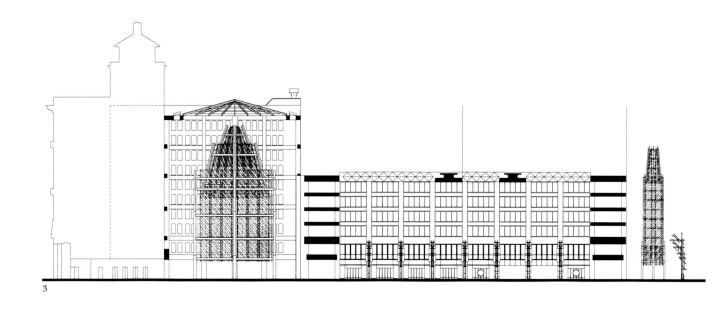

3

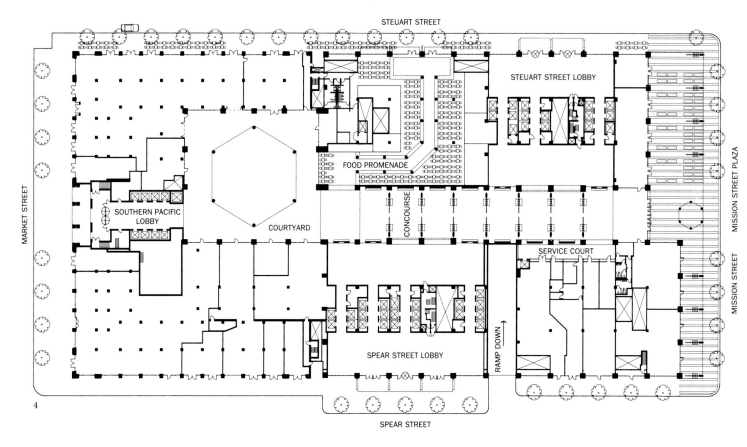

STEUART STREET

STEUART STREET LOBBY

FOOD PROMENADE

SOUTHERN PACIFIC LOBBY

COURTYARD

CONCOURSE

SERVICE COURT

SPEAR STREET LOBBY

RAMP DOWN

MARKET STREET

MISSION STREET PLAZA

MISSION STREET

SPEAR STREET

4

N

5

6 Section through lattice pavilion
7 Computer generated rendering of lattice
  pavilion interior

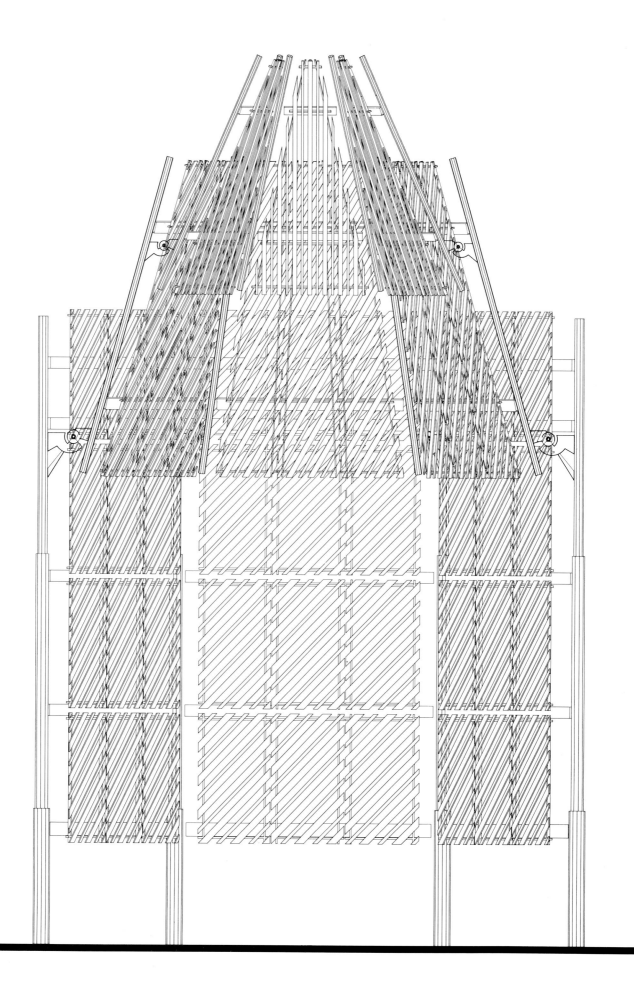

6

8   Computer generated rendering of interior light
      fixtures in concourse
9   Perspective views of light fixtures in interior
      concourse (left), and exterior plaza (right)

8

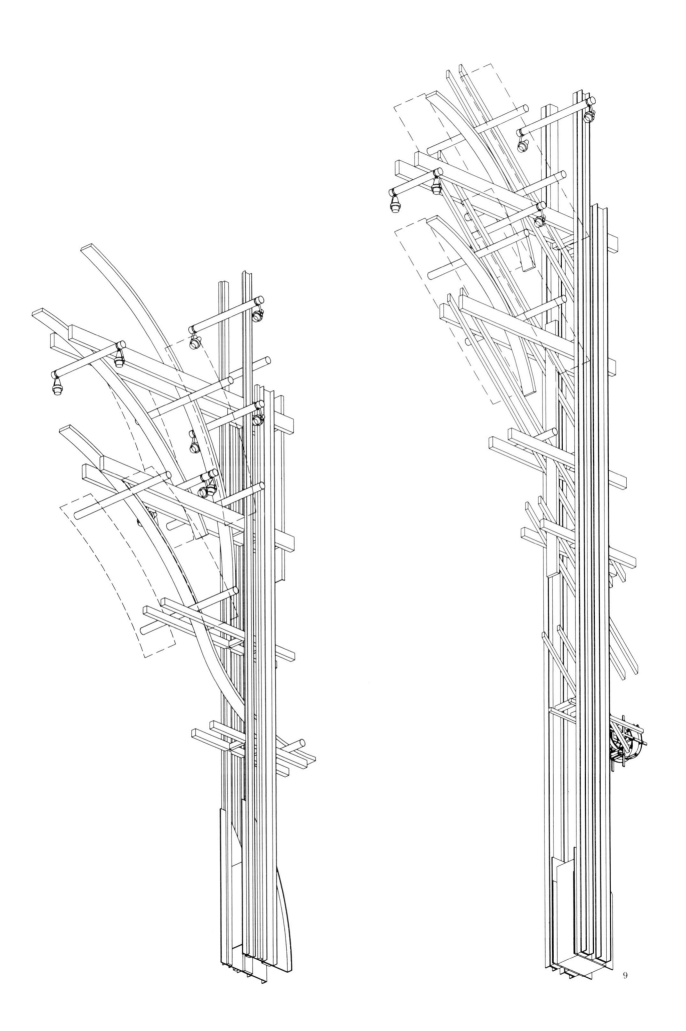

9

Kuala Lumpur City Centre Phase I

Design/Completion 1992/1996
Kuala Lumpur, Malaysia
Kuala Lumpur City Centre (Holdings) Sendirian Berhad
6,000,000 square feet of office space
1,500,000 square feet of retail/entertainment center
Core and cylindrical tube frame system constructed of cast-in-place high-strength concrete. Floor framing on composite steel floor deck and composite rolled steel framing.
Petronas Towers: organized in horizontal ribbons of vision glass and metal

The Kuala Lumpur City Centre is a 97-acre development located in the heart of the commercial district of Kuala Lumpur. Upon completion, it will be a new symbol for the city and the nation.
Phase I of the Kuala Lumpur City Centre development, with a site area of 14.15 acres, will have more than 8 million gross square feet of office space, 1.5 million square feet of retail/entertainment facilities and below-grade parking for 4,500 cars. Other amenities within the complex include a petroleum museum, a symphony hall and a multi-media conference center.

The twin 85-story Petronas Towers, connected by a skybridge at the Sky Lobby level, define an urban gateway of monumental scale. The profile of the towers with their distinctive pinnacles will give the buildings a unique silhouette. The shape of the Petronas Towers floor plate was generated from a conscientious attempt to understand and incorporate Islamic geometric principles, composed of two rotated and superimposed squares with small circular infills.

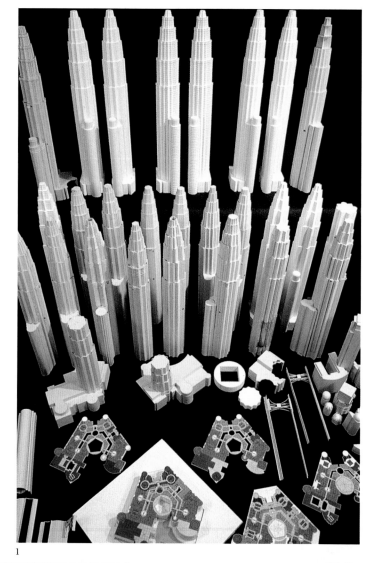

1

2

1 Study models
2 Team members with study models
3 Winning competition model

3

4

5

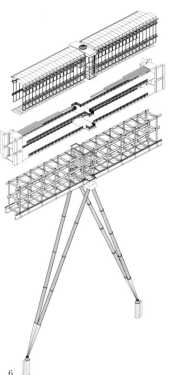

6

4–5 Views of skybridge model
6   Exploded axonometric of skybridge
7   Aerial perspective of towers

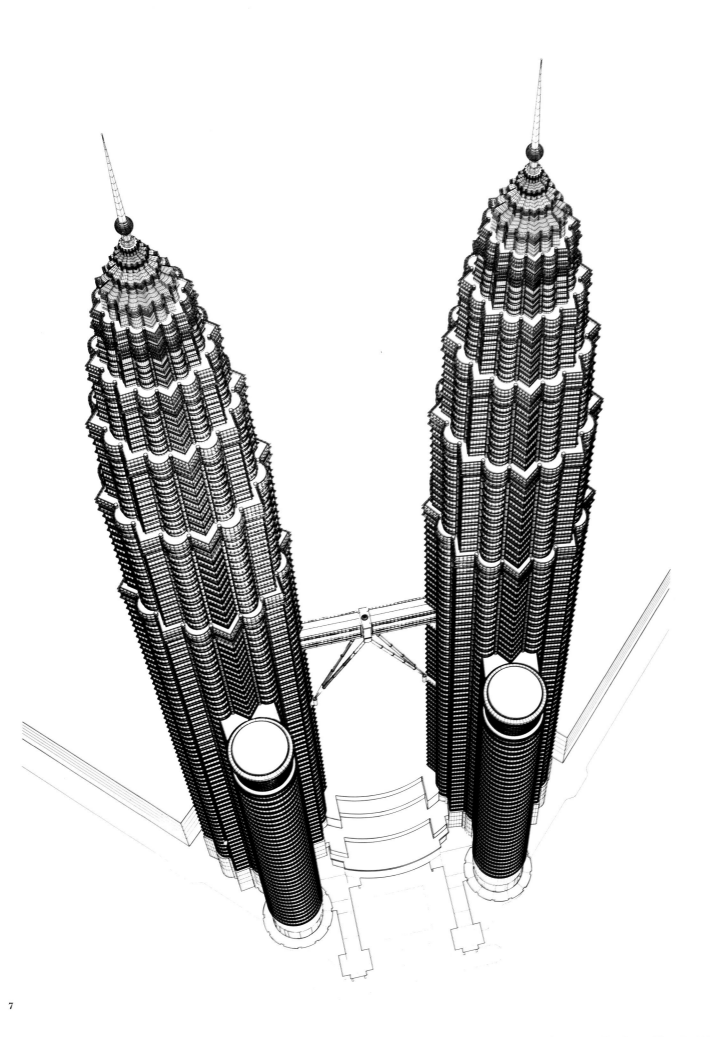

7

8

9

10

11

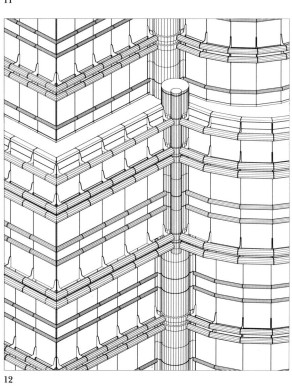

12

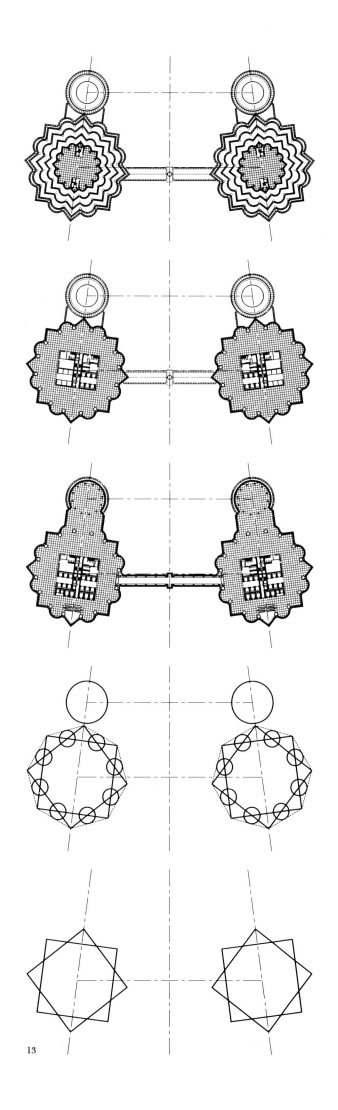

13

11 Model view of curtain wall
12 Axonometric detail of curtain wall setback
13 Generating geometry of tower floorplate
14 Model of center atrium
15 Model of street-level lobby
16 Study of tower base

14

15

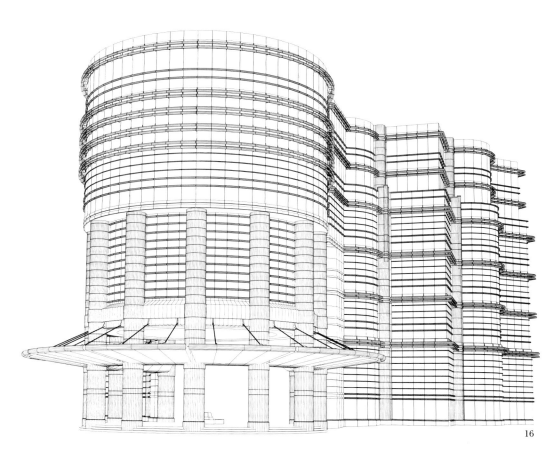

16

17

18

19

20

134

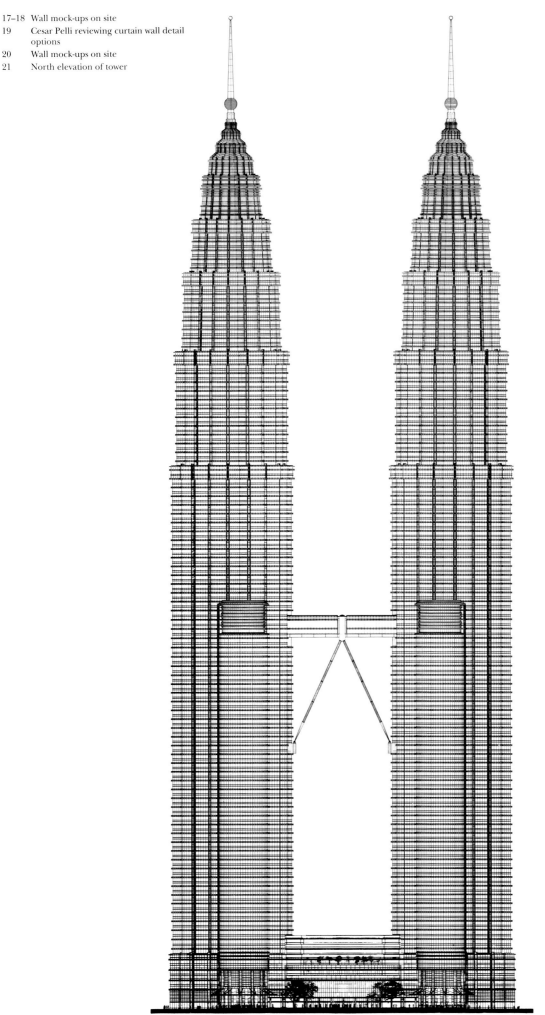

21

Brick

Herring Hall,
Rice University

Design/Completion 1982/1984
Rice University Houston, Texas
Rice University
50,000 square feet
Lightweight steel and brick cavity wall
Brick, limestone and glazed tile

Herring Hall is a good example
of the integration of a new academic
building into an established campus.

The Rice campus, designed in 1910 by
Ralph Adams Cram of Cram, Goodhue
and Ferguson, has a coherent, Beaux-Arts
plan. Herring Hall provides a third wall
of a quadrangle on axis with the central
campus; its composition of shifted, parallel
blocks skewered by arcades and corridors
recalls the organization, typology
and narrow proportions of the first
Rice buildings.

Three separate masses are grouped around
an open court: a three-story building
contains classrooms, administrative facilities
and faculty offices; the west wing contains
the reading room; and the east wing
contains a 250-seat lecture hall.
A circulation spine links the three buildings
on the ground and second floors.

While earlier Rice buildings have carved
stone entrance portals, layered to express
mass, Herring Hall entries are layered
in a way consistent with thin-wall
construction by cutting and folding
the brick skin.

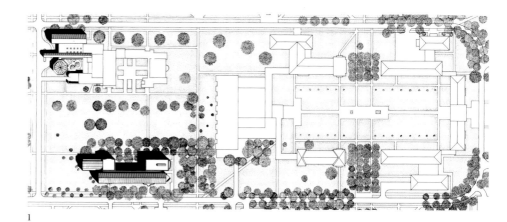

1

2

3

4

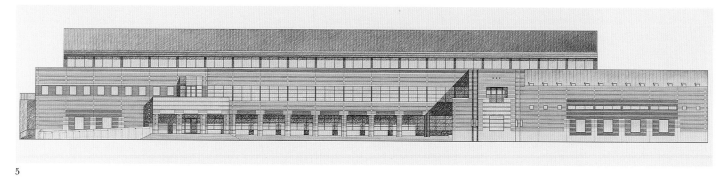

5

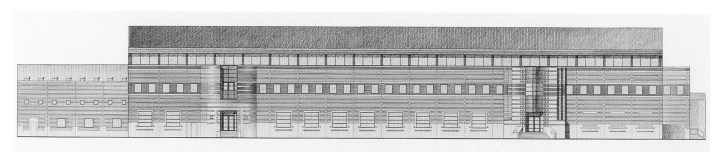

6

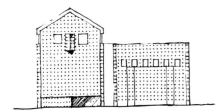
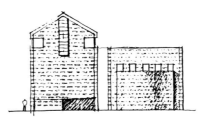
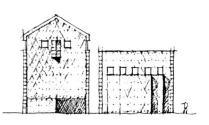

7

8

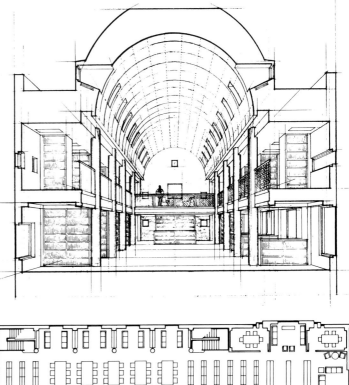

9

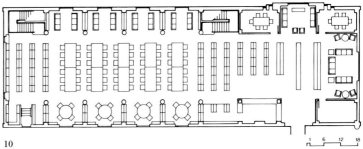

10

11

11 View of main entrance, looking north
12 Southwest entry
13 View of courtyard near entry
14 View south approaching entry

12

13

14

Ley Student Center, Rice University

Design/Completion 1983/1986
Houston, Texas
Rice University
75,000 square feet
Steel frame
Brick with limestone and tile

The expansion of the Ley Student Center fulfilled several crucial campus needs, including the centralization of all student services, and the addition of a bookstore, cafeteria, two private dining rooms, a large lounge and five smaller lounges, an octagonal multi-purpose room and offices for student activity groups.

Referring to existing buildings and the campus plan of 1910 by Cram, Goodhue and Ferguson, its massing consists of long parallel blocks, typical of early Rice buildings. Part of the design intent was to continue the system of expression and ornamentation begun at Herring Hall. Glazed brick, limestone and glazed tile provide rhythms of material change; ornament is used in the surface of the skin to express construction and program. Entrance treatments are layered by cutting and folding the brick skin in a similar way to those of Herring Hall. This method refers to the layered, carved stone portals of earlier Rice buildings while remaining consistent to modern thin-wall construction.

1

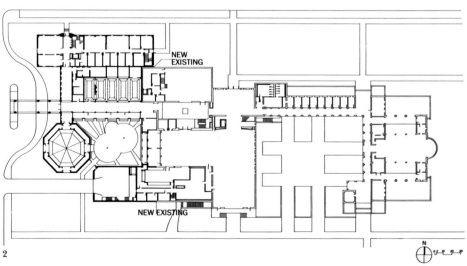

2

1 Lounge area
2 Ground-level plan
3 Detail of interior arcade, view east

3

4 View from west on axis with spine
5 Section, view east
6 Section, view north
7 Axonometric
8–9 Views of courtyard

4

5

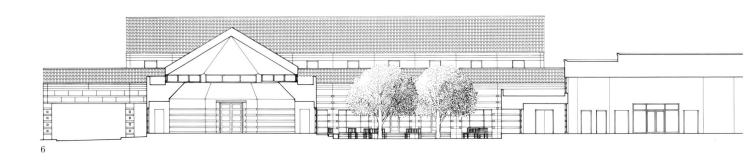

6

146

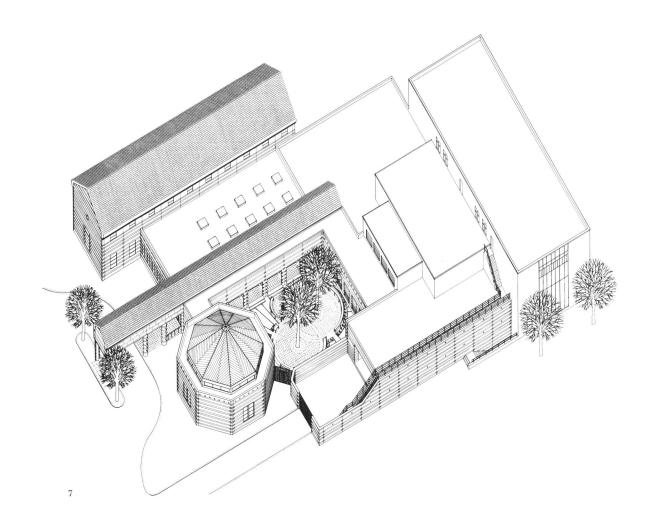

7

8

9

Mattatuck Museum

Design/Completion 1984/1986
Waterbury, Connecticut
The Mattatuck Museum
42,500 square feet
Steel frame
Brick, limestone

The Mattatuck Museum, one
of Connecticut's oldest museums, focuses
on Connecticut history, with collections
ranging from furniture and industrial
artifacts to paintings and works on paper.
The project consisted of the adaptive re-use
of the four-story brick and limestone-clad
Masonic Temple and designs for new
galleries, a 300-seat performance and
conference space, research library, cafe,
classrooms and museum store.

As the museum is situated on the corner
of the Waterbury Green, issues of urban
scale and public image were important
considerations in its design. The entrance
was positioned to receive the corner and
align with existing structures. Materials of
the addition match the brick and limestone
of the original building. A small garden
serves as a sculpture court.

1

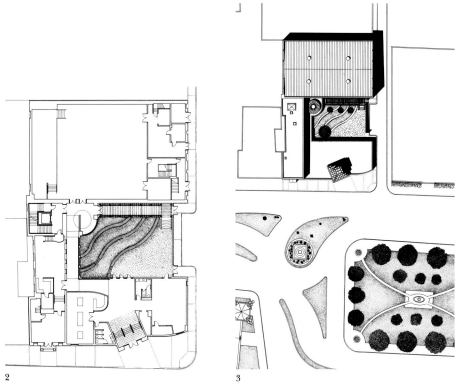

2   3

1   Rendering
2   First-floor plan
3   Site plan
4   View of main entry

148

4

5 Detail
6 Gallery space
7 South elevation

6

7

Boyer Center for Molecular Medicine, Yale University

Design/Completion 1985/1991
New Haven, Connecticut
Yale University School of Medicine,
Howard Hughes Medical Institute
148,000 square feet
Concrete frame with pan joist
Orange/red brick, gray and black brick accents,
limestone, precast concrete

The Boyer Center for Molecular Medicine
is a research facility for advanced study
in genetics and molecular biology.
The Center is organized along a linear
corridor with laboratory space opposite
offices and support areas. Its linear form
creates a visual boundary, following
the curve of College Street.

The four-story research wing has
laboratories on the street side of a double-
loaded corridor, and offices and laboratory
support facing the rear. The administrative
wing contains a lobby, conference
and seminar rooms and offices.

The building's architectural detail,
proportions and scale were designed
in response to the Georgian character
of surrounding medical school buildings.
The facade is articulated by 30-foot
structural bays, with horizontal emphasis
achieved by alternating brick and stone
bands. In contrast to the tautness of the
front, the rear folds onto itself, and is
broken by projections for offices and a stair.

1

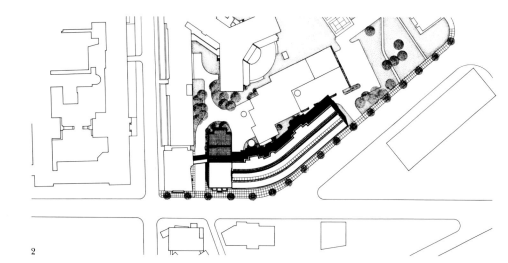

2

1 Rendering of entrance
2 Site plan
3 Dawn view with Hope Building

152

Brick Boyer Center for Molecular Medicine, Yale University   153

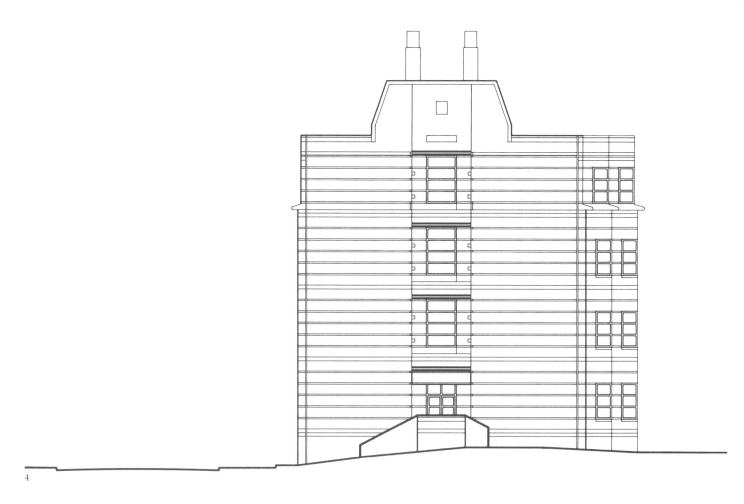

4

5

4　East elevation
5　Dawn view west
6　West elevation
7　View from southwest showing entrance and
　pedestrian bridge

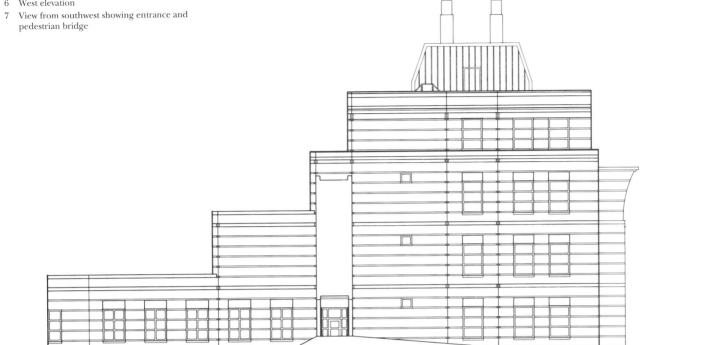

6

7

8

8   View of entrance from second-floor
9   View of entrance area
10 Second-floor plan
11 Ground-floor plan

9

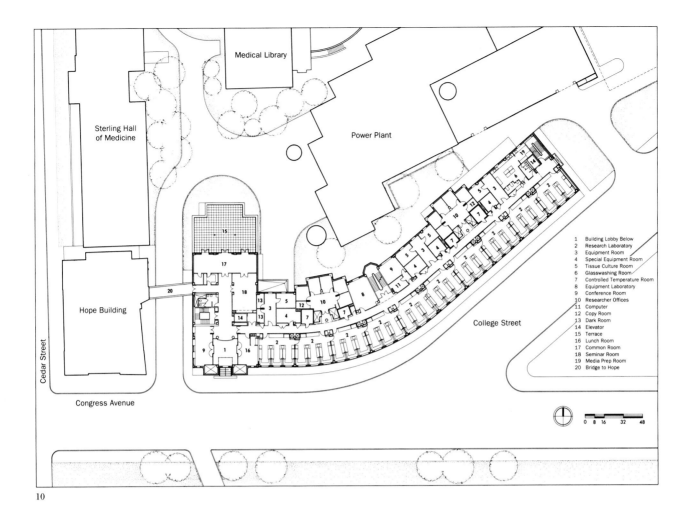

10

Building Lobby Below
1 Building Lobby Below
2 Research Laboratory
3 Equipment Room
4 Special Equipment Room
5 Tissue Culture Room
6 Glasswashing Room
7 Controlled Temperature Room
8 Equipment Laboratory
9 Conference Room
10 Researcher Offices
11 Computer
12 Copy Room
13 Dark Room
14 Elevator
15 Terrace
16 Lunch Room
17 Common Room
18 Seminar Room
19 Media Prep Room
20 Bridge to Hope

11

1 Building Lobby
2 Research Laboratory
3 Equipment Room
4 Special Equipment Room
5 Tissue Culture Room
6 Glasswashing Room
7 Controlled Temperature Room
8 Equipment Laboratory
9 Conference Room
10 Researcher Offices
11 Computer
12 Copy Room
13 Dark Room
14 Elevator
15 Administration Offices
16 Lunch Room
17 Receiving Area
18 Bridge Above

12 Pedestrian bridge, view south
13 Entrance
14 Three alternative conceptual sketches by Cesar Pelli
15 North elevation, view west

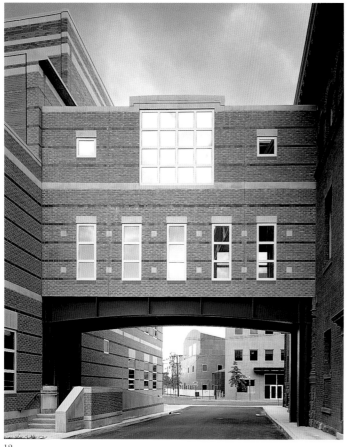

12

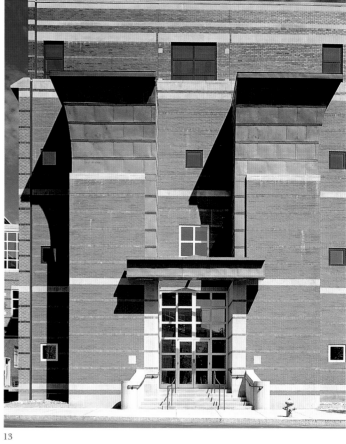

13

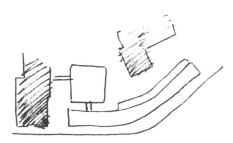

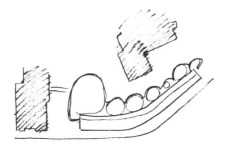

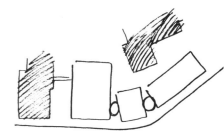

14   spine + pavilion.

spine - 2 sides

3 block.

Brick Boyer Center for Molecular Medicine, Yale University   159

Mathematics, Computing and Engineering Center, Trinity College

Design/Completion 1987/1991
Hartford, Connecticut
Trinity College
49,000 square feet
Steel frame
Red brick, orange glazed brick
Indiana buff limestone sandstone

The Mathematics, Computing and Engineering Center stands on the southern quadrangle of the campus. It is a rectilinear structure, sited to define and create a new quadrangle. A long bar punctuated with end towers, the building responds to the Long Walk, a late 19th century building by William Burges.

Four stories of laboratories, classrooms, seminar rooms, faculty offices and lounges are arranged along a corridor and framed at either end by entrance pavilions. These pavilions are a focus for public activity and campus circulation, both functionally and visually, reinforcing the corners of the quadrangle.

Faculty offices overlook the quadrangle through grouped sets of four windows patterned to relate to older campus buildings. The south elevation is faced with windows in deep vertical recesses that act as sun shields.

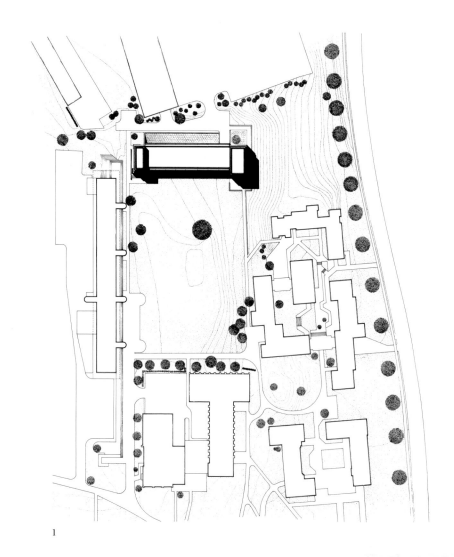

1

2

160

1 Site plan
2 General view of north elevation
3 East tower, view south

3

4 Detail at southeast corner
5 Ground-floor plan
6 View from entrance of north elevation
7 Axonometric

4

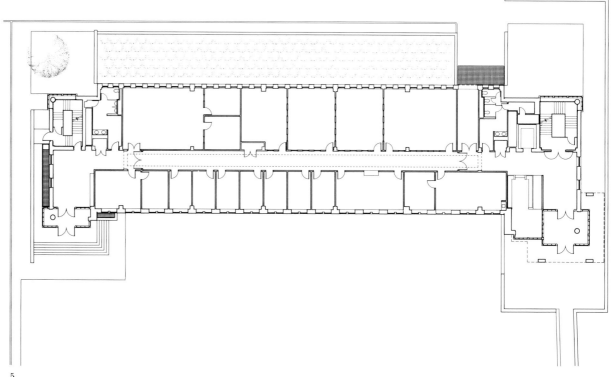

5

6

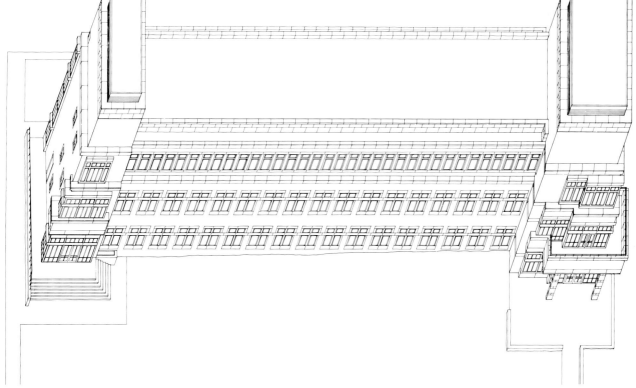

7

8

9

10

11

12

Carnegie Hall Tower

Design/Completion 1987/1991
New York, New York
Rockrose Development Corporation
535,000 square feet
Cast-in-place concrete structural tube
Brick, precast concrete, painted
aluminum cornices, windows and bands

Carnegie Hall Tower is a colorful landmark
on the Manhattan skyline. Using Carnegie
Music Hall's air rights for development,
it was designed as a harmonious addition
to the landmark. Extending the composition
of the Renaissance revival hall, the 60-story
tower reinterprets its massing, coloration
and system of ornamentation.
The hall retained its landmark status
following construction of the tower.

Carnegie Hall Tower is formed
by two interlocking slabs of different sizes.
Elevations are organized similarly to those
of the hall, divided into three parts: two
corner "solids" and a central field. These are
bound together by colored bands at six-story
intervals. The top is a dark frieze beneath
an open metalwork cornice; the shorter
tower has a smaller version of this top.

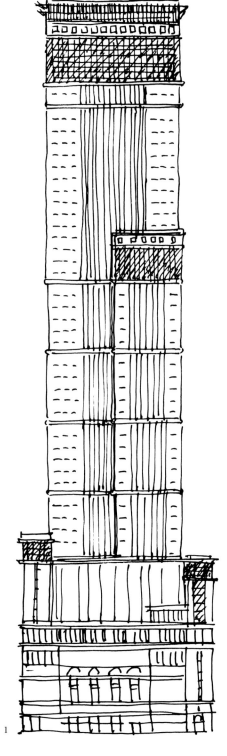

1

Carnegie Tower
- Cesar Pelli 1989

1   Sketch by Cesar Pelli
2   View of Tower from 7th Avenue

166

3

4

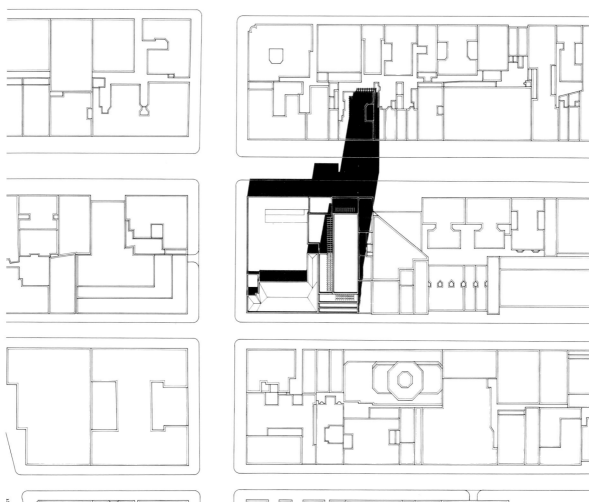

5

6

7 Tower top
8 Study model showing cornice detail
9 Study model of elevation detail
10 57th Street elevation
11 Study model of 57th Street entrance detail
12 General view of Tower

7

8

9

10

11

Century Tower

Design/Completion 1987/1990
New Haven, Connecticut
Century–New Haven Limited Partnership,
Konover/Kenny Associates Inc.
256,000 square feet
Steel frame
Red brick, manganese gray brick,
green Burlington stone

Cesar Pelli & Associates attempted to design
a tower with a character that grows from
the tradition of New Haven and other
New England cities. Century Tower
combines a 19-story office building with
an eight-level parking garage.

Facades are given form by a grid of paired
punched openings in the brick wall.
Windows are delineated by dark green
lintels and center pilasters, and underlined
by common spandrels of dark gray brick.
Windows are larger on the upper three
floors, increasing the proportion of glass
to brick and making the top slightly more
reflective. The entrance is marked by
a gridded lobby wall of sand-finish,
light green Burlington stone.

1

1   General view of Tower, view northeast
2   Rendering of west elevation

3   View of Tower and city
4   Ground-floor plan
5   View of Tower from Church Street
6   Entrance
7   General view south

3

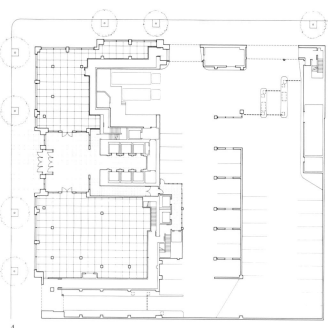

4

5

6

Worrell Professional Center for Law and Management, Wake Forest University

Design/Completion 1989/1993
Winston-Salem, North Carolina
Wake Forest University
185,000 square feet
Steel frame
Virginia brick, sandstone, limestone and copper

The Worrell Professional Center for Law and Management combines the School of Law and the Babcock School of Management in the largest single building on the Wake Forest campus. The first single building to jointly house a law and business school in the United States, its forms and materials were designed to be sympathetic with the architectural tradition of the Wake Forest Campus.

A 55,000 square-foot library is shared by both schools, as well as lounges, classrooms, a technical center and administrative offices. A rotunda with clerestory lighting marks the library, situated between two three-story wings that accommodate classrooms and offices for each school.
The 3.5-acre courtyard is a major landscaped space for the two schools. An arcade lines the perimeter of the courtyard on the ground floor, defining an informal meeting place.

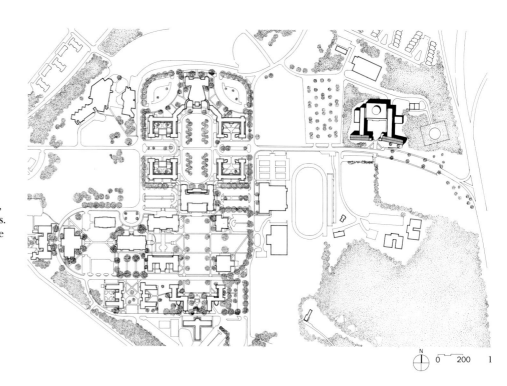

1

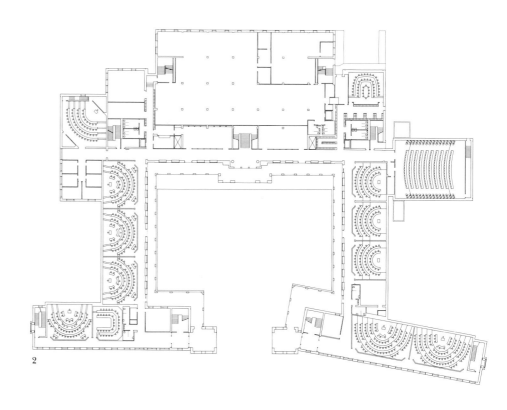

2

1 Site plan
2 Ground-floor plan
3 View of entrance courtyard
4 View from campus entrance

3

4

5

6

7

8

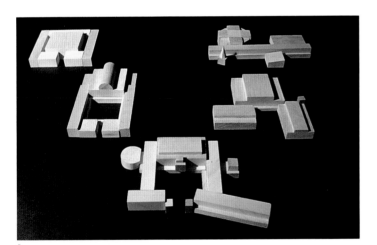

9

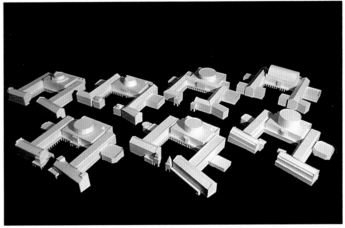

10

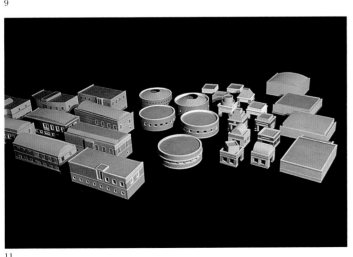

11

12

13 Library rotunda stair
14 Library rotunda ceiling
15 Section through library and courtyard
16 Night view of courtyard
17 Entry into courtyard

13

14

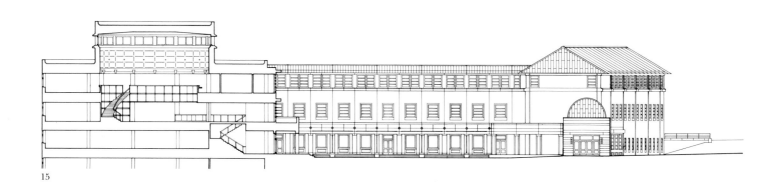

15

16

17

Physics and Astronomy Building, University of Washington/Seattle

Design/Completion 1989/1994
Seattle, Washington
University of Washington/Seattle
265,000 square feet
Steel frame
Multi-colored brick with cast stone
accents and copper panels

The Physics and Astronomy Building provides laboratories, offices, classrooms, computer facilities, four auditoria, a planetarium and a library. The building consists of four architectural components that form a semi-enclosed courtyard: a six-story tower to the west; a four-story horizontal building to the north; a two-story structure to the south-east; and a single-story basement platform on which all the buildings rest, which emerges on grade at the west due to the natural slope of the site. These four components are placed in response to new and existing campus axes. A courtyard will be the major outdoor public space for this part of the campus.

The building forms and details relate to the campus and its building traditions. The planetarium and largest auditorium are emphasized with argyle patterns similar to those found on existing buildings.

An exterior colonnade reinforces the tall, linear auditoria lobby space. Adjacent to this lobby, a large circular stair to the planetarium is contained in a tall glass structure from which suspends a Foucault pendulum.

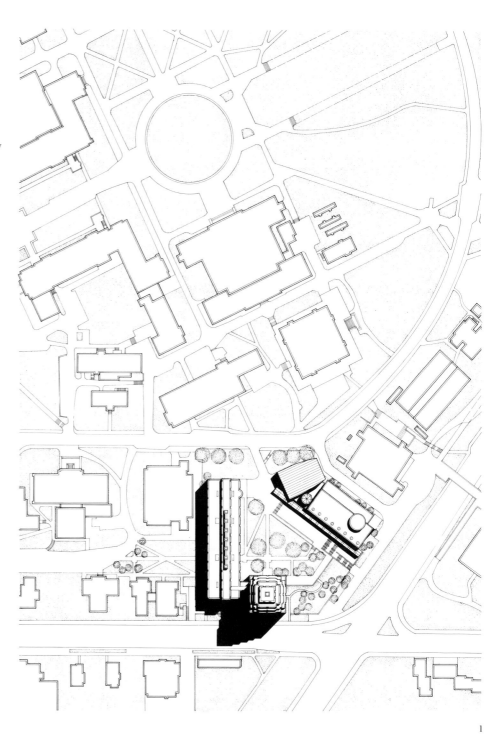

1   Site plan
2   Model view from southwest
3   First-floor plan
4   Foucault pendulum stair structure

2

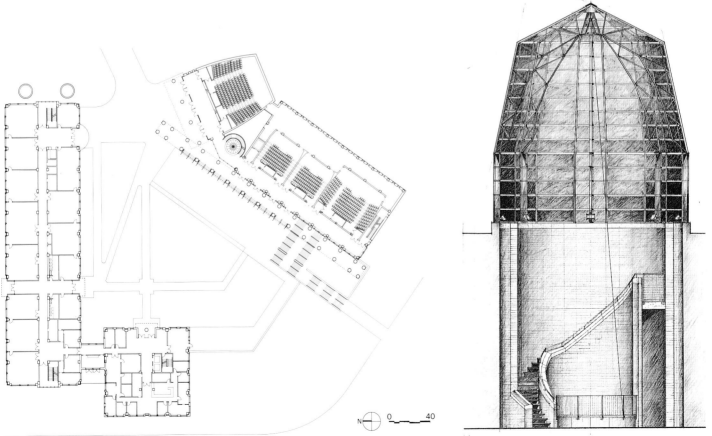

3

4

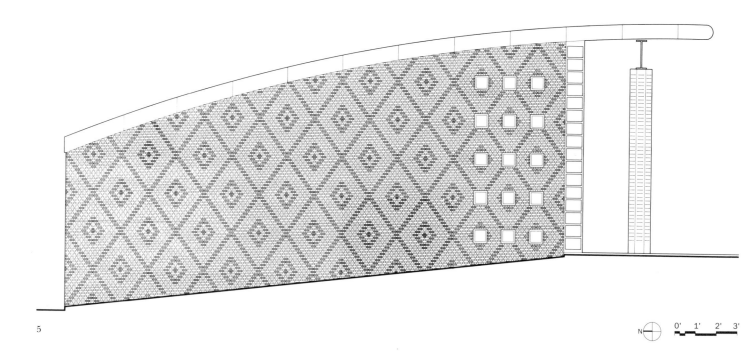

5

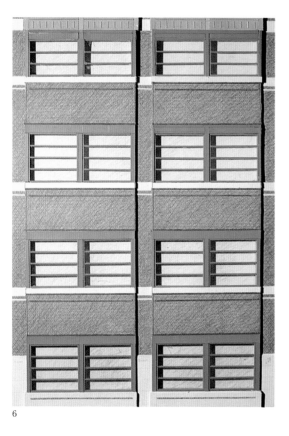

6

7

8

9

10

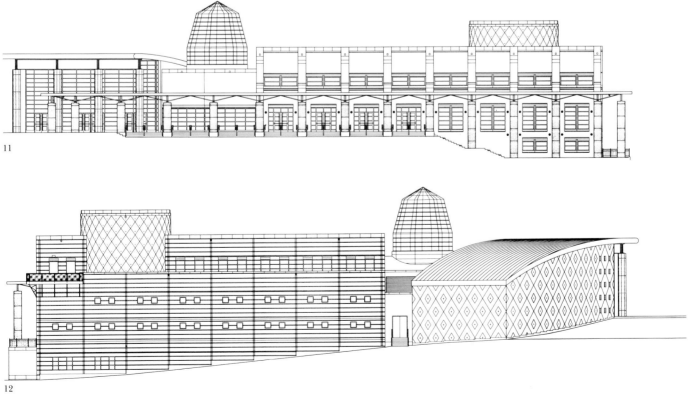

11

12

Frances Lehman Loeb Art Center, Vassar College

Design/Completion 1989/1993
Poughkeepsie, New York
Vassar College
56,500 square feet (27,500 square foot
new addition, 29,000 square foot renovation)
Steel frame
Limestone, pale pink brick

The Frances Lehman Loeb Art Center combines the academic requirements of teaching art history with the exhibition and support requirements of a major regional museum. The Art Gallery is a new building which contains exhibition, conservation and storage spaces, office spaces and two classrooms. The renovated Taylor Van Ingen Hall, a Collegiate Gothic building of 1915, houses the art history department and includes classrooms, offices, study rooms and a slide library.

The center responds to its position in the larger context of Vassar College by creating an edge to the main campus quadrangle and establishing a presence along Raymond Avenue, the most public face of the campus. Viewed from campus, the gallery is a two-story bar with a pitched copper roof that relates directly in form and materials to Taylor Van Ingen Hall. From Raymond Avenue, the two-story bar, the high single story of the galleries and the sculpture garden wall are seen as gentle layers of stone and brick walls—situated to highlight and frame the existing building.

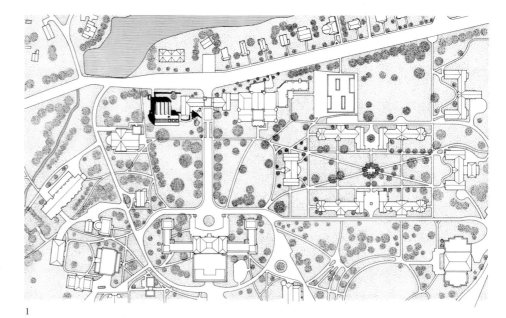

1

2

1 Site plan
2 Entrance courtyard
3 Axonometric drawing
4 Ground-level plan

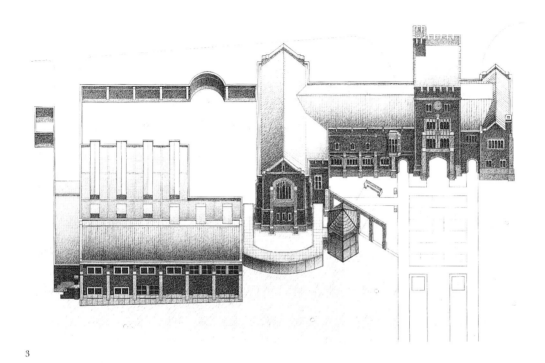

3

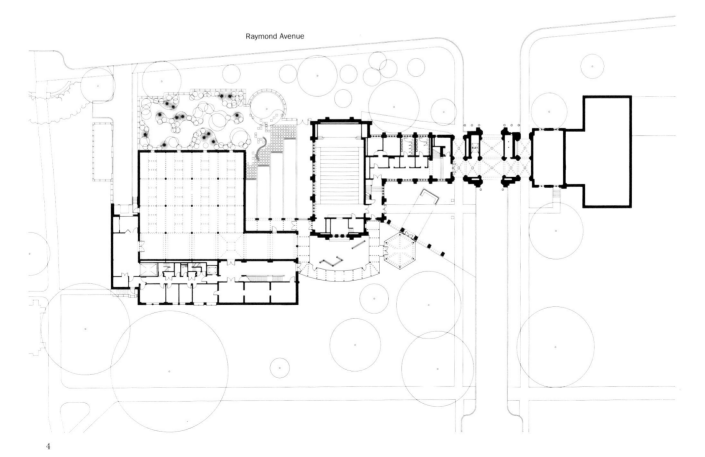

Raymond Avenue

4

5 View of Gallery from Raymond Avenue
6 East elevation
7 Section through galleries and pavilion
8 South elevation
9 View from Raymond Avenue

5

6

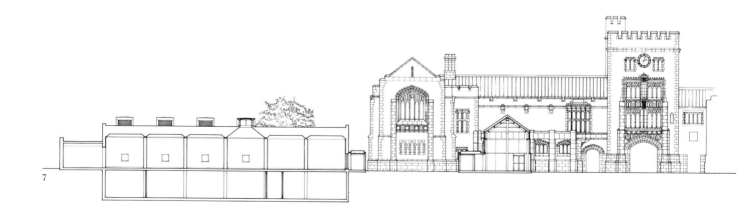

7

188

8

9

10

10 Gallery space
11 View of dormers in stair hall ceiling
12 Entrance courtyard

11

Mathematics Building and Lecture Hall, Institute for Advanced Study

Design/Completion 1989/1993
Princeton, New Jersey
Institute for Advanced Study
23,000 square feet
Steel frame
Molded brick and cast stone

The Institute for Advanced Study is a private institution dedicated to scholarly work in mathematics, physics, natural and social sciences. Founded in 1930, the Institute has a distinguished faculty and an annually selected group of post-doctoral scholars. Albert Einstein was its first permanent faculty member.

The design relates to both the older buildings of the Institute and newer, larger scale buildings on the periphery. The complex comprises two buildings. The 230-seat Wolfensohn (lecture and concert) Hall is finished with exposed wood trusses and wood panelling. The Mathematics Building provides office space for the faculty, computer and secretarial support, a 70-seat classroom, a seminar room and a common room.

The siting of the Mathematics Building creates a courtyard delineated by flowering cherry trees.

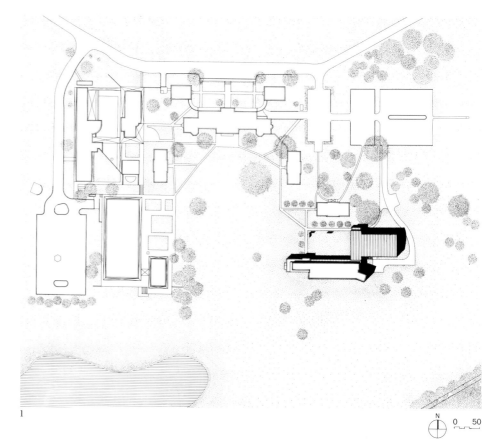

1

2

3

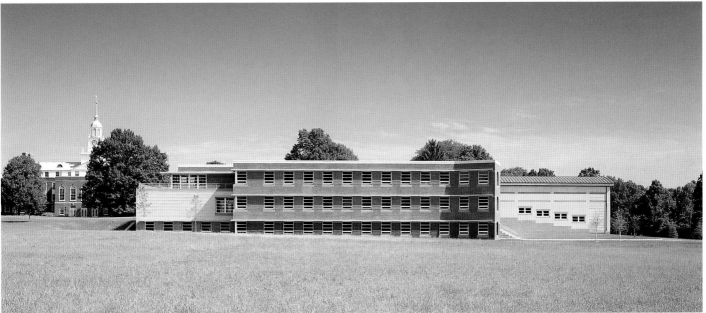

4

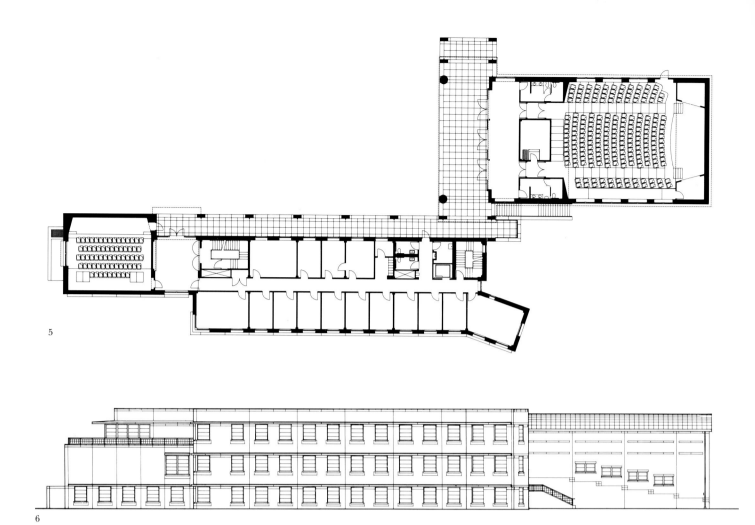

5

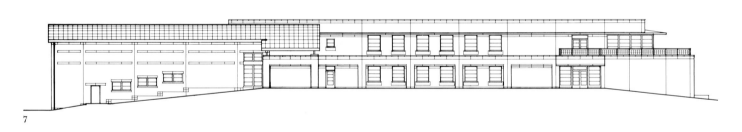

6

7

8

194

9

10 Detail of Lecture Hall porch truss
11 Lecture Hall lobby
12 Lecture Hall interior, view to rear
13 Lecture Hall interior, view to stage

11

12

13

Humanities and Social Sciences Building, University of California/Riverside

Design/Completion 1991/1995
Riverside, California
University of California/Riverside
107,000 square feet
Steel frame
Brick, stucco, cast stone, metal roof

The building marks the west end of the campus. It is a strong composition designed to strengthen and enhance the adjoining Carillon Mall.

The four parallel three-story wings, two transverse two-story wings and square seven-story history tower create three exterior spaces: a courtyard connecting the Fine Arts Mall and the existing Barns, an open-ended court facing Sproul Hall and a small enclosed daylight court within the east transverse wing. These spaces are linked by open colonnaded passageways, weaving the building into the campus. The tower and courtyard gateway of paired stair towers establish a distinct architectural focal point at the south end of the proposed Fine Arts Mall, anchoring future long-range development along that axis.

Detailed in response to the southern Californian climate, with broad roofs in the tradition of early 20th century California bungalows, the building is composed to harmonize with the scale and materials of the campus.

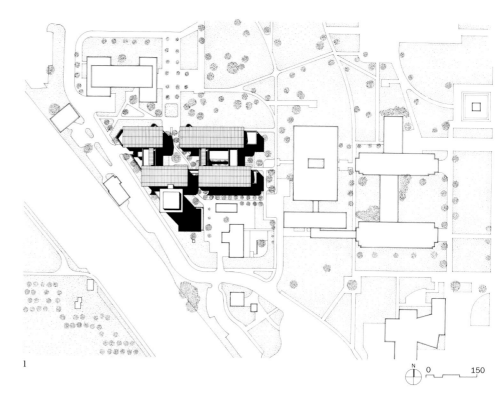

1

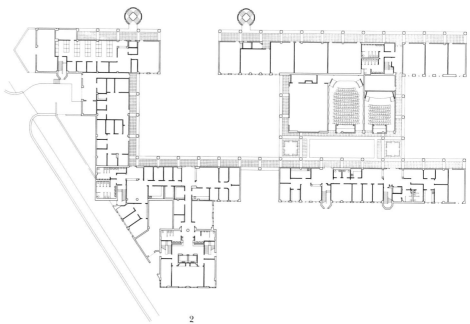

2

3

4

5   Study model showing stair towers,
    view into courtyard
6–7 Detail study models
8   Rendering of history tower and office wings

5

6

7

8

North Carolina Blumenthal Performing Arts Center

Design/Completion 1987/1992
Charlotte, North Carolina
North Carolina Performing Arts Center
at Charlotte Foundation
190,000 square feet
Concrete frame
Brick, stainless steel and glass entry and canopy

The North Carolina Blumenthal Performing Arts Center is part of a mixed-use complex in Center City Charlotte which includes the 60-story NationsBank Corporate Center Tower and Founders Hall, a public room. The Performing Arts Center is the new permanent home of the Charlotte Symphony, Opera Carolina, the Charlotte Repertory Theatre and the Charlotte City Ballet. The center consists of the 2,100-seat Belk Theater, the 450-seat Booth Playhouse, the Rehearsal Hall/Studio Theater and public, performer and staff support spaces.

The exterior takes on the shapes of the spaces it encloses, with different shades of brick finishes and ornamental stringcourses marking them. The two flylofts rise out of the building mass, with that of the Booth Playhouse projecting slightly over College Street. Pedestrian arcades line College Street and Fifth Street. Interior spaces are indicated on the facade through different window types: a screen of openings for offices, a large bow window for the Belk Theater lobby and a rising corner window following a stairway.

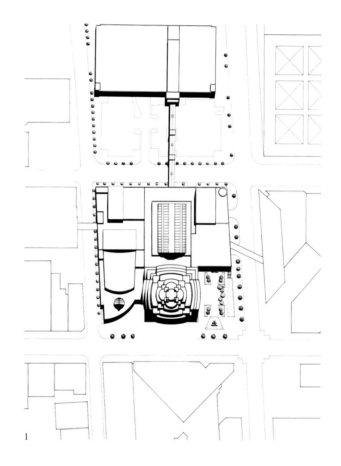

1

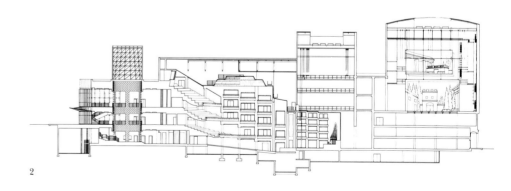

2

1 Site plan
2 Section through large theater lobby, large theater, small theater stage
3 (Top left) Mezzanine/skywalk level
4 (Top right) Balcony
5 (Bottom left) Orchestra/stage/loading level
6 (Bottom right) Grand tier/plaza level

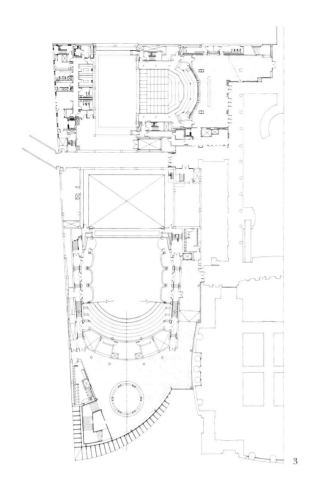

3

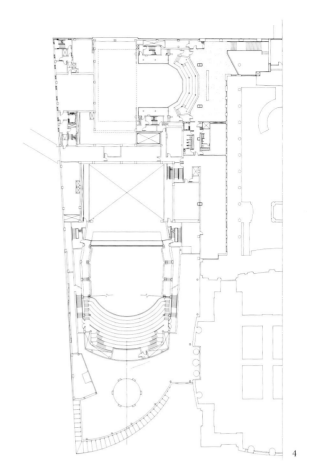

4

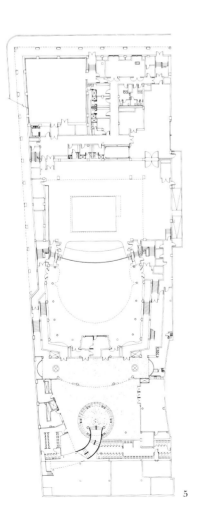

5

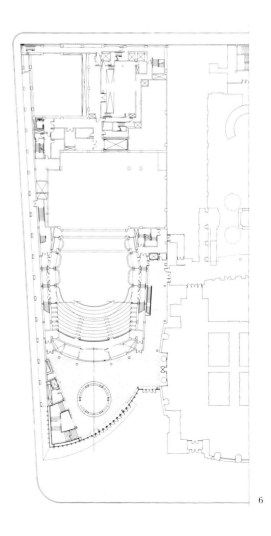

6

7–8 Small theater
9   Exterior of small and large theater flylofts
10   View from corner of College and Fifth Streets

7

8

9

10

11

12

13

14

11–14 Large theater interior

15

16

17

15 Tyron Street facade with view into lobby
16 Facade view from corner of Fifth and Tyron Streets
17 Detail of entrance
18 Facade detail showing stainless steel colonnettes and
   glass canopy

Ohio Center for the Arts—Cincinnati

Design/Completion 1991/1995
Cincinnati, Ohio
State of Ohio, Ohio Building Authority
215,000 square feet
Steel frame
Brick, Minnesota limestone, slate, glass
and stainless steel entry curtain wall

The Ohio Center for the Arts is situated
in the entertainment district of Cincinnati.
The center consists of a 2,700-seat large
theater, 440-seat small theater,
a studio theater and rehearsal hall,
exhibition space and public, performer
and support spaces.

The exterior is two architectural characters
woven together as one composition.
Performance spaces and lobbies have
a civic scale and are contained between
giant masonry walls of brick and stone.
Metal-frame building forms with stone
and glass infill panels enclose additional
programmatic elements which have small
urban scale and character. The entire
composition is tied together with a 14-foot
high stone base and colonnade. The urban
context is enlivened by a colonnade
at street level giving access to theater lobby
entrances, retail shops, stage door and
support staff entrances. The use of the
masonry, brick and stone, and metal-frame
building elements with infill panels responds
to the building traditions and materials of
Cincinnati.

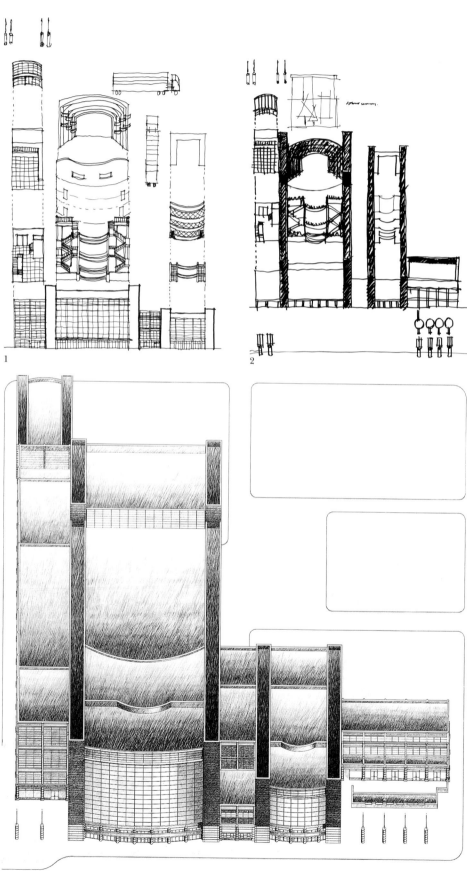

1

2

3

4

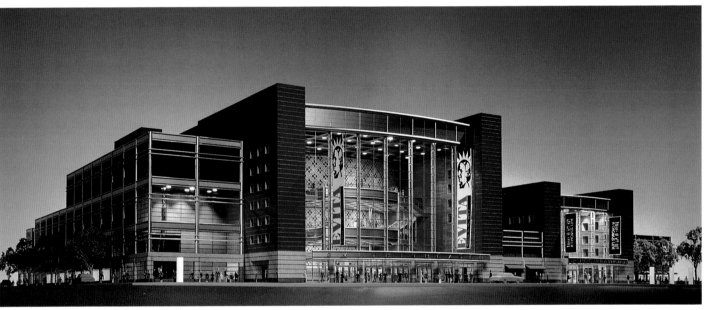

5

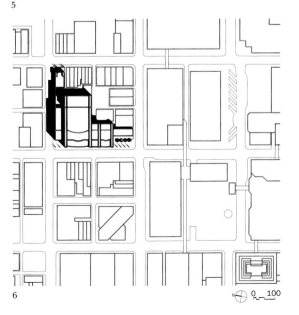

6

1–2 Conceptual diagrams
3 Oblique view
4 Day view of model
5 Night view of model
6 Site plan

N 0 100

7

8

9

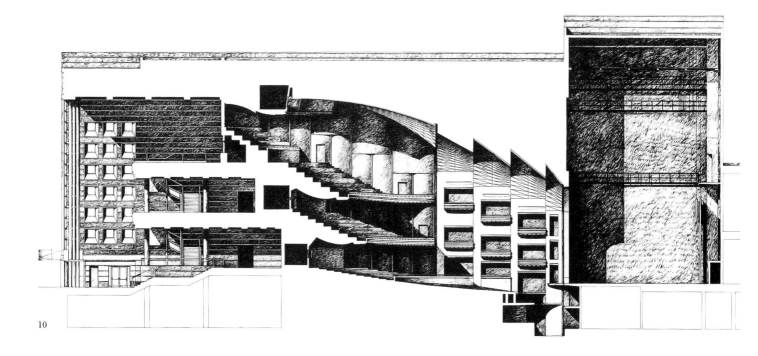

10

7 Model of small theater interior, view to stage
8 Model of large theater interior, view to stage
9 Model of large theater interior showing fiber optically lit ceiling
10 Section drawing through large theater lobby, theater and stage
11 Street/orchestra level plan

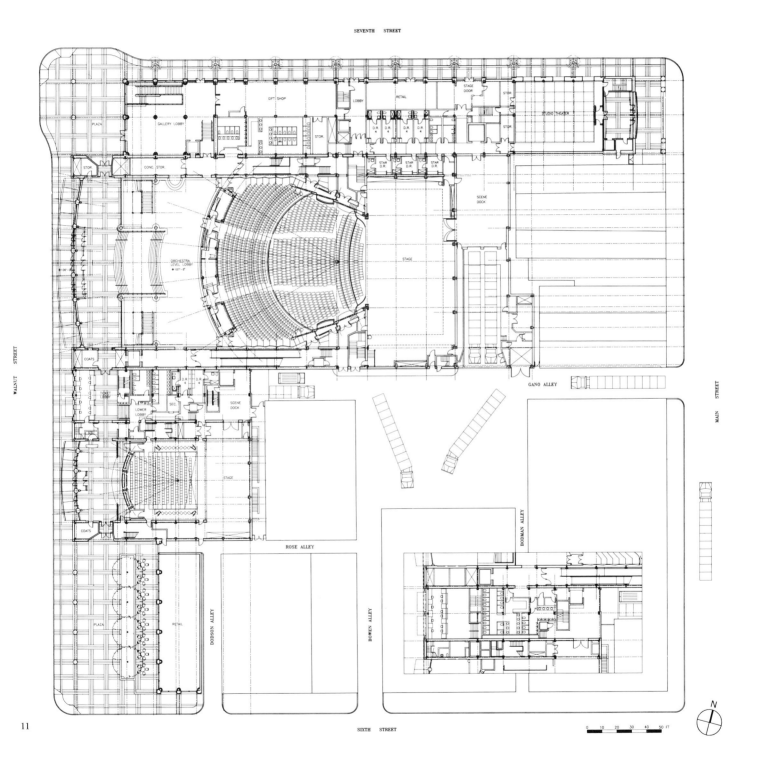

11

Hakata Bay Oriental Hotel and Resort

Design/Completion 1991/1995
Fukuoka City, Japan
Fukuoka Daiei Real Estate Inc.
1,500,000 square feet
Tower: steel frame
Base: reinforced concrete
Tower: ceramic tile and glass (precast concrete panel)
Base: ceramic tile and glass (cast-in-place concrete)

The design for the 35-story, 1,000-room hotel creates a strong sculptural form and memorable image at the edge of Fukuoka City facing Hakata Bay. It is the second of three buildings to be constructed as part of the Twin Dome City Master Plan. The prow-like form of the hotel tower composes with the fractured curved shapes of the baseball stadium and proposed Fantasy Dome in a unified design and establishes a distinct skyline.

The hotel tower stands at the edge of a composition consisting of the curved-wall entrance and glass-roofed cornucopia-shaped Crystal Garden. The luminous Crystal Garden is a vaulted atrium space with fountains, trees, a monumental stair and a freestanding "treehouse" for viewing the interior and bay beyond. Other elements at the base of the hotel include a wedding chapel, lobby lounge and outdoor and indoor pools. Landscape design is integral to the overall design, with exterior gardens creating an atmosphere of rest and gentle civility.

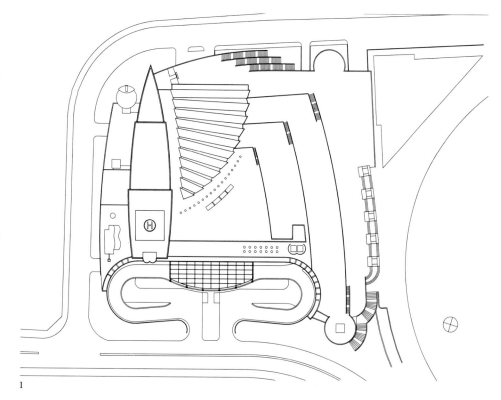

1

2

214

3

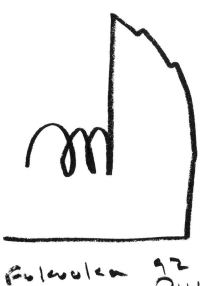

4

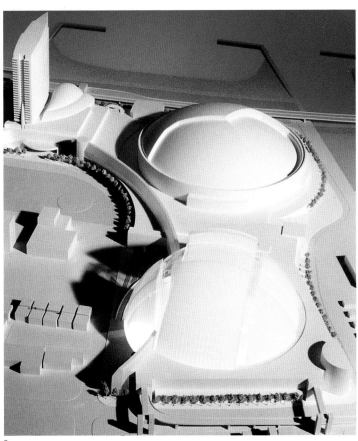

1   Main-floor plan
2   Aerial view of site
3   View of model from the north
4   Sketch by Cesar Pelli
5   Master plan model

5

6

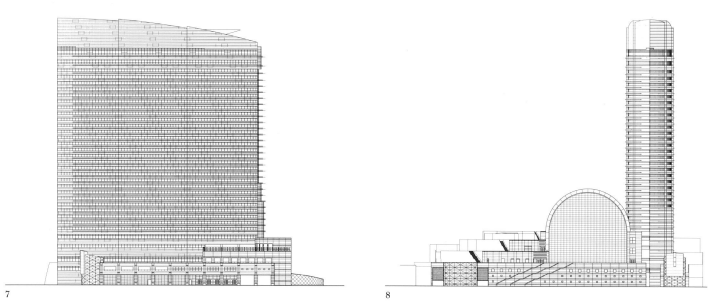

7

8

9

10

6 View of model from the west
7 West elevation
8 North elevation
9 View of model from the southwest
10 View of master plan model from Hakata Bay

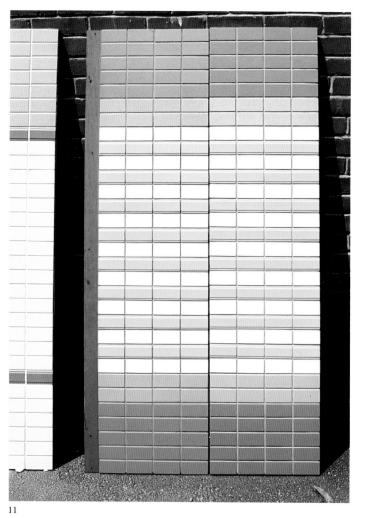

11

12

13

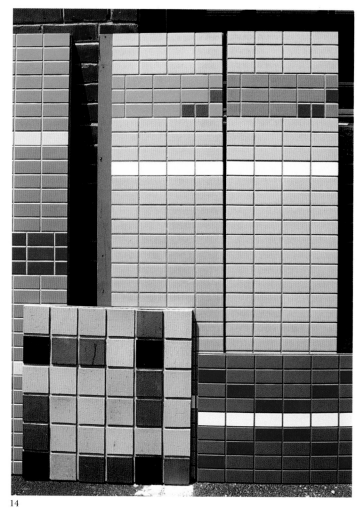

14

15

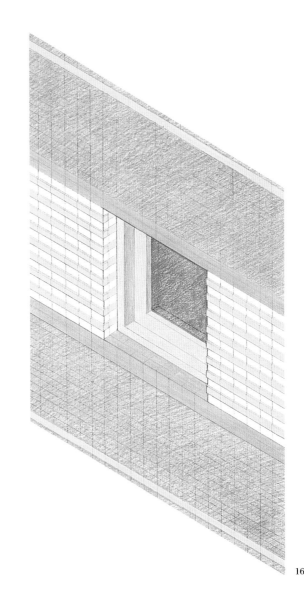

16

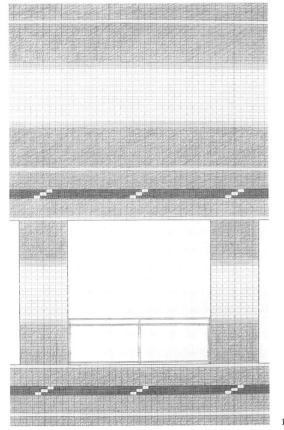

17

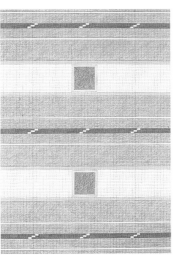

18

11–14 Tile pattern mock-ups
15–18 Elevation studies of main entry tile wall

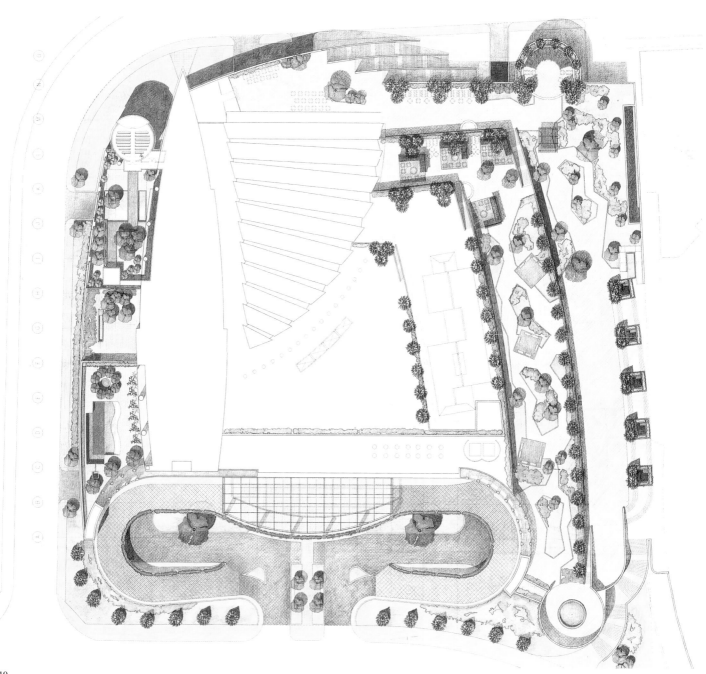

19

19 Landscape plan
20 Main floor plan showing major interior spaces

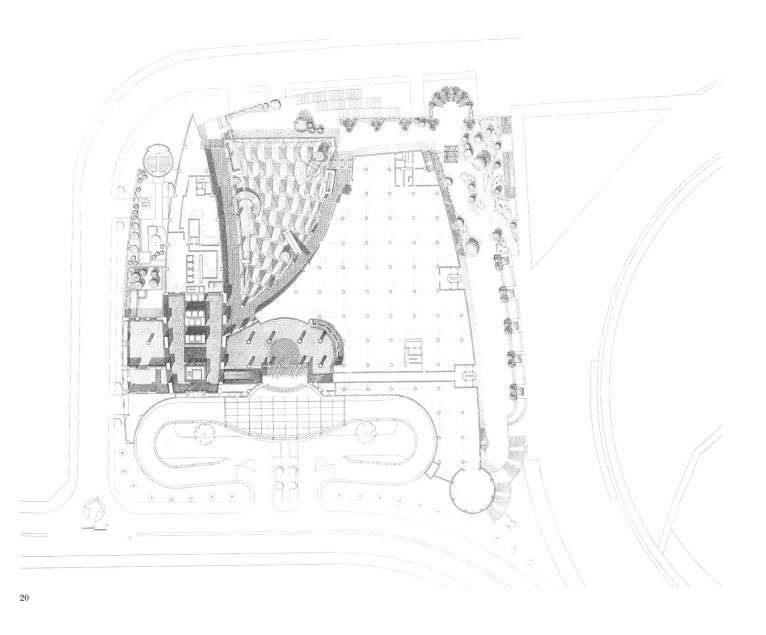

20

21

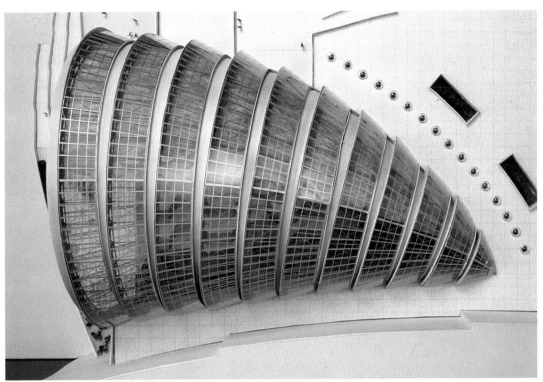

23

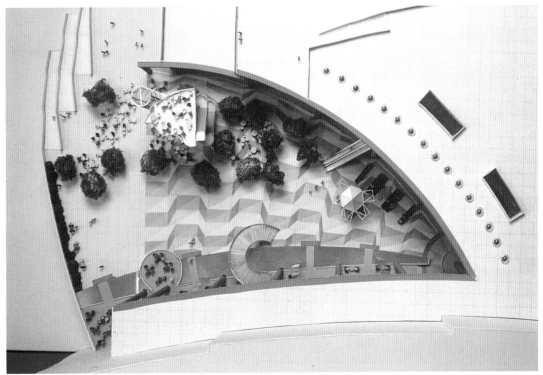

24

21 Rendering of lobby
22 View of lobby model
23 Crystal Garden vault model
24 Crystal Garden study model

25

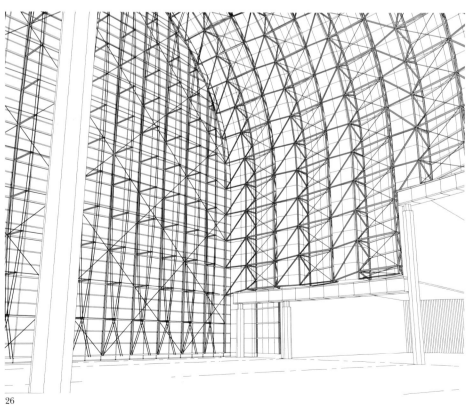

26

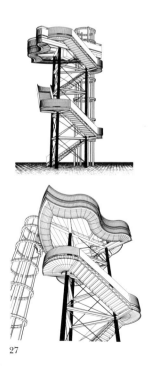

27

28

Biographies

Cesar Pelli
Principal

Cesar Pelli was born in Argentina where he earned a Diploma in Architecture from the University of Tucuman. He came to the United States with a scholarship to attend the University of Illinois, where he received a Master in Architecture. For the next 10 years he worked in the offices of Eero Saarinen, serving as Project Designer for several buildings including the TWA Terminal at JFK Airport in New York and Morse and Stiles colleges at Yale University.

From 1964 to 1968 Cesar Pelli was Director of Design at DMJM (Daniel, Mann, Johnson & Mendenhall) in Los Angeles, and from 1968 to 1976 he was Partner for Design at Gruen Associates in Los Angeles. During this time he designed several award–winning projects, including the San Bernardino City Hall in San Bernardino, California; the Pacific Design Center in Los Angeles, California; and the US Embassy in Tokyo.

In 1977 Mr Pelli became Dean of the Yale University School of Architecture. In the same year he founded Cesar Pelli & Associates. Mr Pelli resigned as Dean of the School of Architecture in 1984, but continues to lecture on architecture. Since the firm's establishment, Mr Pelli has personally originated and directed the design of each of its projects.

Mr Pelli has avoided formalistic preconceptions in his designs. He believes that the aesthetic qualities of a building should grow from the specific characteristics of each project, such as its location, its construction technology and its purpose. In searching for the most appropriate response to each project, his designs have covered a range of solutions and materials.

Mr Pelli's work has been widely published and exhibited, with five books and several whole issues of professional journals dedicated to his designs and theories. He is a Fellow of the American Institute of Architects, an Academician in the American Academy of Arts and Letters, a member of the National Academy of Design and of the Board of Governors of *Perspecta* magazine and a recipient of the Arnold M. Brunner Memorial Prize. He is the first architect to receive a Connecticut State Arts Award.

In 1989 Cesar Pelli & Associates received the AIA Firm Award from the American Institute of Architects. In 1991 the AIA selected Mr Pelli as one of the 10 most influential living American architects. His design of the World Financial Center and Winter Garden at Battery Park City in New York has also been ranked as one of the 10 best works of American architecture since 1980.

Fred Clarke
Principal

Fred W. Clarke, founding Principal, established Cesar Pelli & Associates in 1977 with Cesar Pelli. Mr Clarke acts as a Project Principal and collaborating designer for the firm. He is also responsible for the development of the firm's structure, its unique systems of project organization and delivery and its overall management.

He met Cesar Pelli in 1969 while still a student. In 1970, upon graduating with highest honors from the University of Texas at Austin, he went to work at Gruen Associates in Los Angeles where Mr Pelli was Partner for Design. During the following seven years, Mr Clarke served as Senior Designer and Associate for the US Embassy in Tokyo, Japan; the School of Music for Yale University in New Haven, Connecticut; and the headquarters for the Daehan Kyoyuk Insurance Company in Seoul, Korea.

Upon receiving the commission to design the Museum of Modern Art Gallery Expansion and Renovation, Mr Clarke joined Cesar Pelli in founding the firm in New Haven, Connecticut. Over the past 16 years, Mr Clarke has been project principal and collaborator with Mr Pelli on projects that have included hospitals, research laboratories, academic buildings, museums, performing arts centers, office towers, airports and large-scale mixed-use complexes in the USA and countries around the world.

Mr Clarke has taught in the architecture schools of the University of California at Los Angeles (1972 to 1976) and at Rice University in Houston, Texas (1976). He also served as Visiting Critic in Architecture at Yale University (1977 to 1982), and continues as Guest Critic at Harvard, Princeton and Rice universities, the VIII Bienal de Arquitectura de Quito and the University of Texas, where he was appointed to the Regents Advisory Council of the School of Architecture. Mr Clarke has chaired design juries and professional panels for the Urban Land Institute and the American Institute of Architects.

In 1992 Mr Clarke was elected to the College of Fellows of the American Institute of Architects.

Rafael Pelli
Principal

Rafael Pelli first worked for Cesar Pelli & Associates from 1979 to 1981; he rejoined the firm in 1989. He is currently Design Team Leader for the Radiation Effects Research Foundation headquarters building in Hiroshima, Japan. He is also Design Team Leader for the Hakata Bay Oriental Hotel and Resort in Fukuoka, Japan. The new 34-story hotel will contain 1,000 rooms. It includes the glass vaulted, cornucopia-shaped Crystal Garden facing Hakata Bay, in addition to retail and convention facilities, restaurants and a health club. Construction is under way and is scheduled for completion in 1995.

Prior to these assignments, Rafael Pelli was Senior Designer for Comerica Center in Detroit, Michigan, and for Peachtree Triangle in Atlanta. He also worked as a designer on the Ley Student Center at Rice University, Hermann Park Towers, in Houston, Texas, and the Crile Clinic Building at the Cleveland Clinic.

Before rejoining the firm, Rafael Pelli was a project architect for Hardy Holzman Pfeiffer Associates in New York City from 1986 to 1989. He also privately designed two houses in the town of Seaside, Florida, one of which was featured in *Abitare 267* (July–August 1989).

He taught in Harvard University's Career Discovery Architecture Program in 1985, and served as Guest Critic for Design reviews at the University of Cincinnati in 1986, and at the Parsons School of Design in New York City in 1986 and 1987.

He received a Bachelor of Arts in 1978 from Yale University and a Master of Architecture in 1985 from the Harvard University Graduate School of Design.

Design Credits

**Urban Nucleus
(Cesar Pelli at Daniel, Mann,
Johnson and Mendenhall),** p. 19
Architect: Daniel, Mann, Johnson and
Mendenhall, Los Angeles. Director
of Design: Cesar Pelli; Design Collaborator:
Anthony Lumsden; Project Designer:
Philo Jacobson.

**San Bernardino City Hall
(Cesar Pelli at Gruen Associates),**
pp. 22–23
Architect: Gruen Associates, Los Angeles.
Partner for Design: Cesar Pelli; Project
Principal: Dan Brannigan; Project Designer:
Roylance Bird.

**UN City
(Cesar Pelli at Gruen Associates),** pp. 24–25
Architect: Gruen Associates, Los Angeles.
Partner for Design: Cesar Pelli; Designers:
Roylance Bird, Richard Dodson,
Arthur Golding, Friedrich Kastner,
Doug Meyer, Victor Schumacher,
Engelbert Zobel.

**Commons of Columbus (Cesar Pelli at
Gruen Associates),** pp. 26–27
Architect: Gruen Associates, Los Angeles.
Partner for Design: Cesar Pelli; Project
Co-ordinator: Antal Borsa; Project Designer:
Roylance Bird; Designer:
Victor Shumacher.

**Niagara Falls Winter Garden
(Cesar Pelli at Gruen Associates),** pp. 28–29
Architect: Gruen Associates, Los Angeles.
Partner for Design: Cesar Pelli; Project
Principal: Beda Zwicker; Project Designer:
Gary Engel; Landscape Architect:
M. Paul Friedberg & Partners.

**The Museum of Modern Art Gallery
Expansion and Renovation,** pp. 30–31
Design Architect: Cesar Pelli & Associates.
Design Principal: Cesar Pelli; Project
Principals: Fred Clarke, Diana Balmori;
Design Team Leader: Tom Morton; Project
Architect: Malcolm Roberts; Designers:
Mac Ball, Ken Champlin, Brad Fiske,
Leslie Lu, Mark Schlenker.

Associate Architects: Gruen Associates,
PC, New York (Museum); Edward Durell
Stone Associates, New York (Tower);
Richard Weinstein (planning concept).

Four Leaf/Four Oaks Towers, pp. 32–33
Design Architect (Four Leaf): Cesar Pelli
& Associates. Design Principal: Cesar Pelli;
Project Principal: Fred Clarke; Designers:
Randall Mudge, Kevin Hart, William Butler,
Turan Duda.
Associate Architect (Four Leaf): A.C. Martin
& Associates and Melton Henry Company,
Houston.
Design Architect (Four Oaks): Cesar Pelli &
Associates. Design Principal: Cesar Pelli;
Designers: Douglas Denes, Kevin Hart,
Mitchell Hirsch, Mariko Masuoka.
Associate Architect (Four Oaks):
Melton Henry Company, Houston.

**Pacific Design Center (Phase I)
(Cesar Pelli at Gruen Associates)
Pacific Design Center Expansion
(Phases II and III),** pp. 34–37
Architect (Phase I): Gruen Associates.
Partner for Design: Cesar Pelli; Project
Principals: Edgardo Contini,
Allen Rubenstein; Project Designer:
Miloyko Lazovich.

Design Architect (Phases II and III):
Cesar Pelli & Associates. Design Principal:
Cesar Pelli; Landscape Principal:
Diana Balmori; Design Team Leaders:
Mac Ball, Douglas Denes; Project Managers:
Lily Del Carmen Berrios, Jeff Paine;
Designers: Philip Koether, Susan Papadakis,
Roger Schickedantz; Landscape Designers:
Peter Viteretto, Alan Saucier.

Associate Architect (Phases II and III):
Gruen Associates, Los Angeles.

St Luke's Medical Tower, pp. 38–41
Design Architect: Cesar Pelli & Associates.
Design Principal: Cesar Pelli; Project
Principal: Fred Clarke; Design Team Leader:
Mark Shoemaker; Designers:
Mark Outman, Benjamin Schrier.

Associate Architect: Kendall/Heaton
Associates, Houston.

**US Embassy, Tokyo
(Cesar Pelli at Gruen Associates),** pp. 44–45
Architect: Gruen Associates, Los Angeles.
Partner for Design: Cesar Pelli; Project
Designer: Arthur Golding; Project Manager:
Rolf Sklarek; Designer: Fred Clarke.

Crile Clinic Building , pp. 46–47
Design Architect: Cesar Pelli & Associates.
Design Principal: Cesar Pelli; Project
Principal: Fred Clarke; Landscape Principal:
Diana Balmori; Project Manager:
Bruce Sielaff; Design Team Leader:
F. Macnaughton Ball, Jr.; Designers:
James Baird, Rafael Pelli, Mariko Masuoka.

Associate Architect: Dalton, van Dijk,
Johnson, & Partners
Project Principal: Piet van Dijk

Norwest Center/Gaviidae Common,
pp. 48–53
Design Architect (Norwest Center):
Cesar Pelli & Associates. Design Principal:
Cesar Pelli; Project Principal: Fred Clarke;
Design Team Leader: Jon Pickard; Project
Manager: Malcolm Roberts;
Designers: Gregg Jones, Roberto Espejo,
Greg Jacobson, Tony Markese,
Michael Duddy.

Associate Architect (Norwest Center):
Kendall/Heaton Associates, Houston.

Design Architect (Gaviidae Common):
Cesar Pelli & Associates. Design Principal:
Cesar Pelli; Project Principal: Fred Clarke;
Design Team Leader: Jon Pickard;
Designers: Kristin Hawkins, David Chen,
Michael Hilgeman, Greg Jacobson, Doug
McIntosh, Michael Petti, Michael Duddy.

Design of Skybridge: Cesar Pelli
in collaboration with Siah Armajani.

Architect-of-Record (Gaviidae Common):
Lohan Associates, Chicago, Illinois.

World Financial Center and Winter Garden,
pp. 54–63
Design Architect: Cesar Pelli & Associates.
Design Principal: Cesar Pelli; Project
Principal: Fred Clarke; Landscape Principal:
Diana Balmori; Project Managers:
Tom Morton, Jeff Paine; Design Team
Leader: Jon Pickard; Senior Designers:
Mark Shoemaker, Turan Duda,
Gregg Jones; Designers: Mitchell Hirsch,
Ann Marie Baranowski, Julann Meyers,
Robert Pulito, Lily Del Carmen Berrios,
Cassie York, Walter Miller, Lawrence Ng,
Bradford Fiske, Douglas Denes,
Cheryl Flota, Thomas Soyster,
Chris Williams, David Leonard,
Eric Liebmann.

Associate Architects: Adamson Associates,
Toronto; Haines Lundberg and Waehler,
New York.

World Financial Center Plaza, pp. 54–63
Designed by Cesar Pelli in collaboration with artists Siah Armajani and Scott Burton and landscape architect Paul Friedberg.
Design/Project Principal:
Diana Balmori; Project Managers:
Tom Morton, Jeff Paine; Design Team Leader: Jon Pickard; Designers:
Michael Cadwell, Douglas Denes,
Turan Duda, Mitchell Hirsch.

NationsBank Corporate Center and Founders Hall, pp. 64–71
Design Architect: Cesar Pelli & Associates.
Design Principal: Cesar Pelli; Project Principal/Design Collaborator:
Fred Clarke; Design Team Leader:
Turan Duda; Designers: Paul Bormann,
Julia Hawkinson, Barbara Endres,
Christopher Hays, Masa Ninomiya,
Roberto Espejo, Yann Poisson,
John DaSilva, David M. Strong,
Charlotte Breed.

Landscape Design: Balmori Associates,
New Haven.

Architect-of-Record: HKS Inc., Dallas.

Society Center, pp. 72–75
Design Architect: Cesar Pelli & Associates
Design Principal: Cesar Pelli;
Project Principal: Fred Clarke; Design Team Leaders: Robert Charney,
Mark Shoemaker; Designers: Philip Koether,
Mark Outman, Sharon McGinnis DaSilva,
Ralph Bierschwale, Rio Minami,
Laura Turlington, Miguel Oks,
Dana Hunter, Yann Poisson.
Landscape Principal: Diana Balmori;
Landscape Designer: Peter Viteretto.

Associate Architect: Kendall/Heaton Associates, Inc., Houston (tower);
Glover-Smith-Bode, Inc., Oklahoma City (hotel); Van Dijk, Johnson & Partners,
Cleveland (bank restoration)

Yerba Buena Tower, pp. 76–77
Design Architect: Cesar Pelli & Associates
Design Principal: Cesar Pelli;
Project Principal: Fred Clarke; Design Team Leader: Jon Pickard; Project Manager:
Jeff Paine; Designers: Christoper Burns,
Allison Ewing, Michael Hilgeman.

Building top designed in collaboration with Siah Armajani. Landscape Principal:
Diana Balmori.

181 West Madison, pp. 78–81
Design Architect: Cesar Pelli & Associates
Design Principal: Cesar Pelli;
Project Principal: Fred Clarke; Design Team Leader: Gregg Jones; Designers:
Bruce Davis, Lazaros Papanikolaou,
Greg Barnell, Anthony Markese.

Architect-of-Record: Shaw and Associates,
Inc., Chicago.

Miglin-Beitler Tower, pp. 82–83
Design Architect: Cesar Pelli & Associates
Design Principal: Cesar Pelli;
Project Principal: Fred Clarke; Design Team Leader: Gregg Jones; Designers:
David Chen, Lazaros Papanikolaou,
Greg Barnell.

Architect-of-Record: HKS Inc., Dallas

**COMSAT Laboratories
(Cesar Pelli at Daniel, Mann, Johnson & Mendenhall),** pp. 86–87
Architect: Daniel, Mann, Johnson & Mendenhall Architects, Los Angeles.
Director of Design: Cesar Pelli;
Designer: Philo Jacobson.

Canary Wharf Tower, Retail and Assembly Building and Docklands Light Railway Station, pp. 88–93
Design Architect: Cesar Pelli & Associates
Design Principal: Cesar Pelli; Project Managers: Thomas Morton, Jeff Paine;
Design Team Leaders: Robert Bostwick,
Lawrence Ng, Robert Taylor,
Lisa Winkelmann; Designers: David Chen,
David Johnson, DeWitt Zuse, Sarah Amelar,
John Apicella, Ruth Bennett, Sunny Evangelista Carroll, Michael Green,
Jong-Gon Kim, Maki Kuwayama,
Julia Parker, Michael Petti, Matthias Richter,
Frank Sheng, David Shklar, Bret Sleeper,
Bettina Stark, Roberta Weinberg,
Masami Yonezawa.

Associate Architect: Frederick Gibberd Coombes and Partners, London;
Adamson Associates, Toronto;
Atkins Sheppard Fidler & Associates,
Surrey, England.

777 Tower, pp. 94–97
Design Architect: Cesar Pelli & Associates
Design Principal: Cesar Pelli;
Project Principal: Fred Clarke;
Design Team Leader: Gregg Jones;
Designers: Marcy Schulte,
Lazaros Papanikolaou,
Greg Barnell, Mariko Masuoka.

Associate Architect: Langdon Wilson Architecture, Planning, Los Angeles.

Plaza Tower, pp. 98–101
Design Architect: Cesar Pelli & Associates
Design Principal: Cesar Pelli;
Design Team Leader: Jun Mitsui; Project Managers: Bruce Sielaff, Cherie Santos;
Designers: Kevin Burke, Scott Aquilina,
Hiroyuki Kataoka, David Toti.

Associate Architect: CRSS Inc., Irvine

NTT Shinjuku Headquarters Building,
pp. 102–107
Architects: Cesar Pelli & Yamashita Associated Architects
Design Architect: Cesar Pelli & Associates
Design Principal: Cesar Pelli; Project Principal: Fred Clarke; Design Team Leaders: Jun Mitsui, Gregg Jones,
David Chen; Designers: Kevin Burke,
Karen Koenig, Masami Yonasawa,
Douglas McIntosh, Roger Schickedantz,
Roberto Espejo, Ruth Bennett,
Scott Aquilina.

Architect-of-Record: Yamashita Sekkei Inc.,
Tokyo.

New North Terminal, Washington National Airport, pp. 108–117
Design Architect: Cesar Pelli & Associates
Design Principal: Cesar Pelli;
Project Principal: Fred Clarke; Design Team Leader: Mark Shoemaker; Project Manager: Phillip Bernstein; Designers:
Anthony Markese, Philip Koether,
Sharon McGinnis DaSilva, David Toti,
Barbara Endres, Michael Green,
Bernard Proeschl, Sunny Evangelista Carroll, Lisa Winkelmann, Issac Campbell,
Philip Nelson, Yann Poisson, Jeanne Smith,
James Winkler, Alison Horne,
Jennifer Carpenter, Dewitt Zuse.
Associate Architects: Leo A. Daly,
Washington; Pierce Goodwin Alexander & Linville, Alexandria

One Market, pp. 118–125
Design Architect: Cesar Pelli & Associates
Design Principal: Cesar Pelli;
Project Principal: Fred Clarke; Design Team Leader: Turan Duda; Designers:
Mariko Masuoka, John DaSilva,
Robert Narracci, David Strong,
Kristin Hawkins, Tim Paxton,
Masa Ninomiya, Roberto Espejo.

Associate Architect: Whisler-Patri,
San Francisco.

**Kuala Lumpur City Centre,
Phase I,** pp. 126–135
Design Architect: Cesar Pelli & Associates
Design Principal: Cesar Pelli; Project
Principal: Fred Clarke; Design Team Leader:
Jon Pickard; Project Manager: Larry Ng;
Designers: Gregg Jones, John Apicella,
David Chen, David Coon, Ed Dionne,
Peter Follett, Fritz Haeg, Mike Hilgeman,
Russell Holcombe, Alison Horne,
Steven Marchetti, Robert Narracci,
Mark Outman, Enrique Pelli,
Roger Schickedantz, David Strong,
Vlad Simionescu, Jane Lareau Twombley.

Architect: Architectural Division,
KLCC Bhd, Kuala Lumpur.

Technical Consultant: Adamson Associates,
Toronto, Ontario.

Interior Consultant: STUDIOS,
San Francisco.

Herring Hall, Rice University, pp. 138–143
Design Architect: Cesar Pelli & Associates
Design Principal: Cesar Pelli; Project
Principal: Fred Clarke; Landscape Principal:
Diana Balmori; Design Team Leader:
Kevin Hart; Project Architect:
Howard Howes; Designer: William Butler.

Ley Student Center, Rice University,
pp. 144–147
Design Architect: Cesar Pelli & Associates
Design Principal: Cesar Pelli; Project
Principal: Fred Clarke; Landscape Principal:
Diana Balmori; Design Team Leader:
Kevin Hart; Project Managers:
Howard Howes, Mark Hesselgrave;
Designers: Mitchell Hirsch,
Gregg Jones, Rafael Pelli;
Landscape Designer: Peter Viteretto.

Mattatuck Museum, pp. 148–151
Design Architect: Cesar Pelli & Associates
Design Principal: Cesar Pelli; Project
Principal: Fred Clarke; Landscape Principal:
Diana Balmori; Design Team Leader:
Mac Ball; Project Manager: Howard Howes;
Designers: Mark Hesselgrave,
Mitchell Hirsch, Peter Tagiuri.

**Boyer Center for Molecular Medicine,
Yale University,** pp. 152–159
Design Architect: Cesar Pelli & Associates
Design Principal: Cesar Pelli; Project
Principal: Fred Clarke; Project Manager:
Bruce Sielaff; Design Team Leader:
Robert Taylor; Project Architects:
Roger Schickedantz, Timothy McGrath;
Designers: Richard Brown, Roberto Espejo,
Mark Hesselgrave, Michael Hilgeman,
Walter Miller, Susan Papadakis,
Benjamin Schreier; Interior Designers:
Julann Meyers, Karen Koenig-Johnson.

Landscape Design: Balmori Associates,
New Haven.

**Mathematics, Computing and Engineering
Center, Trinity College,** pp. 160–165
Design Architect: Cesar Pelli & Associates
Design Principal: Cesar Pelli; Project
Principal: Fred Clarke; Landscape Principal:
Diana Balmori; Project Manager: Jeff Paine;
Design Team Leader: William Butler;
Project Architect: Mark Hesselgrave;
Designers: Tim Paxton, John Apicella,
Roger Schickedantz; Landscape Designer:
Peter Viteretto; Interior Designer:
Julann Meyers.

Carnegie Hall Tower, pp. 166–171
Design Architect: Cesar Pelli & Associates
Design Principal: Cesar Pelli;
Project Principal: Fred Clarke; Design Team
Leader: Kevin Hart; Project Manager:
Malcolm Roberts; Designers:
Mitchell Hirsch; Robert Bostwick,
Mihaly Turbucz, Lisa Winkelmann
Timothy Paxton, Douglas McIntosh.

Architect-of-Record: Brennan Beer Gorman,
New York

Century Tower, pp. 172–175
Design Architect: Cesar Pelli & Associates
Design Principal: Cesar Pelli;
Project Principal: Fred Clarke; Design Team
Leader: Mariko Masuoka; Designers:
David Barkin, Alison Ewing,
Mark Hesselgrave, Masami Yonezawa.

Associate Architect: Stecker, LaBau,
Arneill, McManus Architects Inc.,
Hartford

**Worrell Professional Center for
Law and Management, Wake Forest
University,** pp. 176–181
Design Architect: Cesar Pelli & Associates
Design Principal: Cesar Pelli; Project
Principal: Fred Clarke; Design Team
Leader: Robert Taylor; Project Architect:
Malcolm Roberts; Project Manager:
Philip Bernstein; Designers:
Laura Turlington, Timothy McGrath,
Masaaki Ninomiya, Michael Hilgeman,
Frank Emery, Charlotte Breed,
John Apicella, John DaSilva;
Interior Designer: Julann Meyers.

Landscape Design: Balmori Associates,
New Haven.

**Physics and Astronomy Building, University
of Washington/Seattle,** pp. 182–185
Architect: Cesar Pelli & Associates/NBBJ
Associated Architects

Design Architect: Cesar Pelli & Associates
Design Principal: Cesar Pelli;
Design Team Leaders: Kristin Hawkins,
Kevin Hart; Senior Designer:
Mihaly Turbucz; Designers: J. Bunton,
Robert Taylor, David Toti, Isaac Campbell,
Hirotaka Kataoka.

Associated Architect: NBBJ, Seattle.

**Frances Lehman Loeb Art Center,
Vassar College**
pp. 186–191
Architect: Cesar Pelli & Associates
Design Principal: Cesar Pelli; Design
Collaborator/Project Principal: Fred Clarke;
Design Team Leader:
Patricia MacDougall; Project Architect:
Laura Turlington; Designers: John Apicella,
Isaac Campbell, Craig Copeland,
Michael Hilgeman, Hirotaka Kataoka,
Masaaki Ninomiya, Seiki Tagawa,
James Winkler; Construction
Administration: David Barkin, Jeff Paine;
Interior Designer: Julann Meyers.

Landscape Design: Balmori Associates,
New Haven.

**Mathematics Building and Lecture Hall,
Institute for Advanced Study,** pp. 192–197
Architect: Cesar Pelli & Associates
Design Principal: Cesar Pelli; Project
Manager: Jeff Paine; Design Team Leader:
Mariko Masuoka; Project Architect:
Mark Hesselgrave; Designers:
Steve Marchetti, Masaaki Ninomiya,
Tim Paxton.

Landscape Design: Balmori Associates,
New Haven.

**Humanities and Social Sciences Building,
University of California/Riverside,**
pp. 198–201
Architect: Cesar Pelli & Associates
Design Principal: Cesar Pelli; Project
Principal: Fred Clarke; Design Team Leader:
Robert Taylor; Project Architect: Mark
Hesselgrave; Designers: Seiki Tagawa, James
Winkler, Tim Paxton,
Masaaki Ninomiya.

Landscape Design: Balmori Associates,
New Haven.

North Carolina Blumenthal Performing Arts Center, pp. 202–209
Design Architect: Cesar Pelli & Associates
Design Principal: Cesar Pelli; Project
Principal/Design Collaborator: Fred Clarke;
Design Team Leader:
Mitchell Hirsch; Designers: Keith Krolak,
Mihaly Turbucz, Margarita McGrath,
Suzanne Mitchell, Masaaki Ninomiya.

Architect-of-Record: Middleton,
McMillan Architects Inc., Charlotte.

Associate Architect: Morris Architects,
Houston.

Theater Planner: Theatre Projects
Consultants Inc., Ridgefield.

Acoustician: Kirkegaard Associates,
Donners Grove.

Ohio Center for the Arts—Cincinnati,
pp. 210–213
Design Architect: Cesar Pelli & Associates
Design Principal: Cesar Pelli; Design Team
Leader: Mitchell Hirsch; Designers: Patricia
MacDougall, J. Bunton, Keith Krolak, Kio
Ozawa, Lazaros Papanikolaou,
Jane Twombley.

Architect-of-Record: GBBN Architects,
Cincinnati.

Theater Planner: Theatre Projects
Consultants Inc., Ridgefield.

Acoustician: Kirkegaard Associates,
Donners Grove.

Landscape Design: Balmori Associates,
New Haven.

Hakata Bay Oriental Hotel and Resort,
pp. 214–225
Design Architect: Cesar Pelli & Associates
Design Principal: Cesar Pelli; Project
Principal: Fred Clarke; Design Team
Leaders: Rafael Pelli, William Butler;
Project Director: Jun Mitsui; Designers:
Bruce Davis, David Chen, David Johnson,
Steven Marchetti, Mihaly Turbucz,
Roberta Weinberg, Takahiro Sato,
Hiroyuki Takahara.

Collaborating Architects: Cesar Pelli &
Associates, Environmental Development
Research Inc., Tokyo.

Landscape Design: Balmori Associates,
New Haven.

Associates & Collaborators

Principals

Cesar Pelli
Fred Clarke
Rafael Pelli

Senior Associates

Phillip G. Bernstein
William Butler
Turan Duda
Mitchell A. Hirsch
Gregg E. Jones
Mariko Masuoka
Jun Mitsui
Lawrence S. Ng
Jeffrey L. Paine
Jon Pickard
Mark R. Shoemaker

Associates

Robert L. Bostwick
David P. Chen
Sharon McGinnis DaSilva
Bruce Davis
Kristin Hawkins
Mark S. Hesselgrave
David M. Johnson
Philip Koether
Keith Krolak
Patricia F. MacDougall
Steven J. Marchetti
Anthony J. Markese
Julann Meyers
Mark A. Outman
Malcolm Roberts
Roger Schickedantz
Robert Taylor

Collaborators

John A. Apicella
David H. Barkin
Elizabeth A. Beers
Yvonne M. Bruton
J. Bunton
Kevin Burke
Isaac S. Campbell
Jennifer M. Carpenter
Craig G. Copeland
J. Peter Coracci
Sunny Evangelista Carroll
David Coon
John R. DaSilva
Jerome del Fierro
Edward Dionne
Renée Dobos
Susana L.P. Drago

Barbara Endres
Roberto J. Espejo
Regina Estelle
Peter Follett
Alan M. Gemmell
Jack A. Gold
Michael C. Green
Fritz Haeg
María E. Hernández
Michael Hilgeman
Russell Holcomb
Alison W. Horne
Janet Kagan
Karen Koenig-Johnson
Lisa Masoud
Carolann Morrissey
Robert J. Narracci
Philip Nelson
Masaaki Ninomiya
Dean A. Ober
Kiyohiko Ozawa
Lazaros Papanikolaou
Timothy T. Paxton
Yann L.A. Poisson
Bernard S. Proeschl
Cherie Santos
Takahiro Sato
Hiroyuki Shimizu
Vlad Simionescu
Jeanne Smith
Elizabeth Steele
David M. Strong
Janet N. Tompkins
David Toti
William Traill
Mihaly Turbucz
Laura Pirie Turlington
Jane Lareau Twombly
Marianne Urbano
Andrea Volta
James Winkler
Heather H. Young
Axel Zemborain

Chronological List of Buildings and Projects

*Indicates work featured in this book
(see Selected and Current Works).

Director of Design,
Daniel, Mann, Johnson & Mendenhall
Los Angeles, California

*Urban Nucleus, Sunset Mountain Park
1965
Santa Monica, California
Sunset International Petroleum
Corporation

Jewelers Center
1965–1967
Beverly Hills, California

Roosevelt Building Renovation
1965
Los Angeles, California

Teledyne Laboratories
1966–1968
Northridge, California
Teledyne Systems Corporation

Century City Medical Plaza
1966–1969
Los Angeles, California
Pacific Coast Medical Enterprises

Federal Office Building
1966–1973
Lawndale, California
General Services Administration

**General Telephone Building
and Wilshire West Apartments**
1966–1970
Santa Monica, California
Lawrence Welk Plaza

Kodak Laboratories
1966–1969
Los Angeles, California
Eastman Kodak Company

Ala Wai Plaza
1967–1972
Honolulu, Hawaii
Business Investment, Ltd

Worldway Postal Center
1967–1970
Los Angeles, California
United States Postal Service

St Vincent's Hospital
1967–1975
Los Angeles, California
Daughters of Charity of St Vincent
de Paul

*COMSAT Laboratories
1967–1969
Clarksburg, Maryland
The Communications Satellite
Corporation

Kukui Gardens
1967–1969
Honolulu, Hawaii
Clarence T.C. Ching Foundation

**Bunker Hill Third Street
Tunnel Extension**
1967
Los Angeles, California
City of Los Angeles

California Jewelry Mart
1968
Los Angeles, California

Partner for Design, Gruen Associates,
Los Angeles, California

Pacific Centre
1968–1971
Vancouver, British Columbia
Pacific Center Ltd

*San Bernardino City Hall
1969–1972
San Bernardino, California
City of San Bernardino and the City
Redevelopment Agency

*UN City
1969
Vienna, Austria
City of Vienna, Republic of Austria
Winning competition entry; project

Beef N' Counter
1969
St Louis, Missouri
American Snacks, Inc.

Western Electric Building/Gateway II
1969–1972
Newark, New Jersey
Amterre Corporation

Manchester Lease
1969
Clayton, Missouri
American Snacks, Inc.

**Snowmass at Aspen
Lineal Village-Planning**
1969–1971
Aspen, Colorado
Snowmass American Corporation

*Commons of Columbus
1970–1973
Columbus, Indiana
Irwin Management Inc.

Security Pacific National Bank
1970–1972
San Bernardino, California
Security Pacific National Bank

Laguna Niguel Museum and Cultural Center
1970
Laguna Niguel, California
Laguna Niguel Corporation
Project

Ohrbach's Del Amo
1970
Torrance, California
Ohrbach's Inc.

*Pacific Design Center, Phase I
1971–1975
Los Angeles, California
Sequoia Pacific

Wells Fargo Building
1971–1973
Oakland, California
Bramalea Pacific; Grubb & Ellis
Company

Ohrbach's Cerritos
1971
Cerritos, California
Ohrbach's Inc.

United California Bank
1971
San Jose, California
Wolff Sesnon Development Company

*US Embassy
1972–1975
Tokyo, Japan
US Department of State

Fox Hills Mall
1973
Culver City, California
Ernest W. Hahn Inc.

Clorox Headquarters Building
1973–1975
Oakland, California
Bramalea Pacific; Grubb & Ellis
Company

Zurich American Eastern Zone Headquarters
1973
Moorestown, New Jersey
Zurich-American Insurance Company

Yale School of Music
1974
New Haven, Connecticut
Yale University
Project

Lauritsen Laboratory for Laser Systems Research and Development
1974
China Lake, California
US Navy, Western Division, Naval
Facilities Engineering Command

*Niagara Falls Winter Garden
1975–1977
Niagara Falls, New York
Niagara Falls Urban Renewal Agency

Daehan Kyoyuk Life Insurance Headquarters Building
1976–1979
Seoul, South Korea
Daehan Kyoyuk Life Insurance
Company Ltd

Biennale House
1976
Venice, Italy
Venice Biennale
Exhibition

Principal, Cesar Pelli & Associates
New Haven, Connecticut

*Museum of Modern Art Gallery Expansion and Renovation
1977–1984
New York, New York
Museum of Modern Art/Trust
for the Cultural Resources
of the City of New York

Dravo Building
1978
Pittsburgh, Pennsylvania
Proposal

*Four Leaf Towers
1979–1982
Houston, Texas
Interfin Corporation

Pin Oak Master Plan
1979
Houston, Texas
Pin Oak Development Company
Winning competition entry

Hermann Park Towers
1979
Houston, Texas
Beni Stabili
Winning competition entry; project

Office Building/Bunker Hill Redevelopment
1979
Los Angeles, California
Bunker Hill Associates
Competition entry

Four Stamford Forum
1980–1984
Stamford, Connecticut
F.D. Rich Company Inc.; Stamford New
Urban Corporation

900 Third Avenue
1979
New York, New York
Progress Corporation

State Office Building
1979
Sacramento, California
State of California
Project

***Crile Clinic Building**
1980–1984
Cleveland, Ohio
Cleveland Clinic Foundation

***Four Oaks Towers**
1980–1982
Houston, Texas
Interfin Corporation

Long Gallery House
1980
Leo Castelli Gallery in New York
New York
Exhibition

Indiana Tower
1980
White River Park, Indianapolis, Indiana
White River Park Development
Corporation
Project

Pin Oak One
1980
Houston, Texas
Ayrshire Corporation
Project

***World Financial Center and
Winter Garden**
1980–1989
New York, New York
Olympia & York Equity Corporation
Winning competition entry

Crown Center North Building
1980
Kansas City, Missouri
Crown Center Redevelopment
Corporation
Project

**"Hexagonal Room" Collaboration:
Artists and Architects**
1980
New York, New York
Architectural League of New York
Exhibition

Chicago Tribune Tower
1980
Chicago, Illinois
Museum of Contemporary Art
Exhibition

Museum of Fine Arts Feasibility Study
1981
Austin, Texas
University of Texas

Casa Otoñal Elderly Housing
1981–1986
New Haven, Connecticut

Music School Campus Master Plan
1981
New Haven, Connecticut
Yale University
Project

435 College Street Renovation
1981
New Haven, Connecticut
Yale University

***Herring Hall**
1982–1984
Houston, Texas
Rice University

Humana Office Building
1982
Louisville, Kentucky
Humana Corporation
Competition entry

New Orleans Tower
1982
New Orleans, Louisiana
1984 World Exposition
Project

Center for the Visual Arts
1983
Columbus, Ohio
Ohio State University
Competition entry

ARCORP Town Center Master Plan
1983
Weehawken, New Jersey
Arthur E. Imperatore
Project

East Village Student Apartments
1983–1985
Hartford, Connecticut
University of Hartford

Fiat Lingotto Building
1983
Turin, Italy
Fiat Sp.A.
Exhibition

Rice University Master Plan
1983
Houston, Texas
Rice University

***Ley Student Center**
1983–1986
Houston, Texas
Rice University

***Mattatuck Museum**
1984–1986
Waterbury, Connecticut
The Mattatuck Museum

Belle Isle Master Plan
1984
Oklahoma City, Oklahoma

Art Center
1984
Nimes, France
Competition entry

Fan Pier Master Plan
1984
Boston, Massachusetts
Hyatt Boston; Carpenter Associates
Project

***Pacific Design Center Expansion,
Phases II and III**
1984–1988
Los Angeles, California
Birtcher; Worldwide Realty Corporation;
Santa Fe Pacific Realty

Hudson River Center
1984
New York, New York
Palatine Realty Corporation
Proposal

Maryland Residence
1984–1989
Glen Echo, Maryland

Playa Vista Master Plan
1984
Los Angeles, California

Poydras Tower
1984
New Orleans, Louisiana
Ayrshire Land Dome Joint Venture
Project

High Street Garage Renovation
1984
New Haven, Connecticut
Chapel Investment Company

Museum of Modern Art Feasibility Study
1984
San Francisco, California
San Francisco Museum of Modern Art

***Norwest Center**
1985–1989
Minneapolis, Minnesota
Hines Interests Limited Partnership

Galveston Arch
1985
Galveston, Texas
Mitchell Energy and Development;
J.R. McConnell

Columbus Circle
1985
New York, New York
Rich–Eichner Joint Venture
Proposal

Downtown Urban Design Plan
1985
Hartford, Connecticut
Equity Ventures Inc.

***Yerba Buena Tower**
1985
San Francisco, California
Olympia & York; California Equities
Project

300 West Monroe
1985
Chicago, Illinois
Project

***Boyer Center for Molecular Medicine**
1985–1991
New Haven, Connecticut
Yale University School of Medicine

***Canary Wharf Tower, Retail and
Assembly Building and Docklands Light
Railway Station**
1986–1991
London, England
Olympia & York Canary Wharf Ltd.

***Gaviidae Common**
1986–1989
Minneapolis, Minnesota
Brookfield Development Inc.

***181 West Madison**
1986–1990
Chicago, Illinois
Miglin-Beitler Developments

New Madison Square Garden
1986
New York, New York
Georgetown Properties/Madison Square
Garden Corporation
Proposal

Ukrainian Museum
1986
New York, New York
Ukrainian Museum
Project

Kentucky Botanical Garden
1986
Louisville, Kentucky
Kentucky Botanical Garden
Project

**SunarHauserman Corporate
Headquarters**
1986
Cleveland, Ohio
SunarHauserman Inc.
Project

*Carnegie Hall Tower
1987–1991
New York, New York
Rockrose Development Corporation
Winning competition entry

Society for Savings Bank Tower
1987
Hartford, Connecticut
Society Corporation; Hines Interests
Limited Partnership
Project

*Society Center
1987–1992
Cleveland, Ohio
Richard and David Jacobs Group
Winning competition entry

DeNunzio Swimming Pool
1987–1990
Princeton, New Jersey
Princeton University

*St Luke's Medical Tower
1987–1990
Houston, Texas
St Luke's Episcopal Hospital
Winning competition entry

*777 Tower
1987–1990
Los Angeles, California
South Figueroa Plaza Associates

***NationsBank Corporate Center
and Founders Hall**
1987–1992
Charlotte, North Carolina
NationsBank Corporation; Charter
Properties; Lincoln Property Company

*Century Tower
1987–1990
New Haven, Connecticut
Konover/Kenny Associates;
Century–New Haven Limited
Partnership

***Mathematics, Computing and
Engineering Center**
1987–1990
Hartford, Connecticut
Trinity College

***North Carolina Blumenthal
Performing Arts Center**
1987–1992
Charlotte, North Carolina
North Carolina Performing Arts
Center at Charlotte Foundation

War Memorial
1987
Providence, Rhode Island
Brown University
Competition entry

**Century Executive Park Master
Plan and Office Building**
1987
Rocky Hill, Connecticut
Equity Ventures Inc.

Pennsylvania Station Center
1987
New York, New York
Competition entry

Campus Improvements and Renovations
1987
New Haven, Connecticut
Yale University

**Convention Center Feasibility
Study and Master Plan**
1987
Hartford, Connecticut
City of Hartford

*Miglin-Beitler Tower
1988
Chicago, Illinois
Miglin-Beitler Developments

Wyoming Residence
1988–1992
Jackson Hole, Wyoming

Kansai Airport Passenger Terminal
1988
Osaka, Japan
Kansai International Airport
Company Inc.
Competition entry

School of Nursing Programming Study
1988
New Haven, Connecticut
Yale University

California Lifeguard Station
1988
Los Angeles, California
Kirsten Kiser Gallery for Architecture
Exhibition

***Worrell Professional Center
for Law and Management**
1989–1993
Winston-Salem, North Carolina
Wake Forest University

*Frances Lehman Loeb Art Center
1989–1993
Poughkeepsie, New York
Vassar College

*Plaza Tower
1989–1991
Costa Mesa, California
C.J. Segerstrom and Sons

*Physics and Astronomy Building
1989–1994
Seattle, Washington
University of Washington/Seattle

*Mathematics Building and Lecture Hall
1989–1993
Princeton, New Jersey
Institute for Advanced Study

**Yale University Press Building
Renovation and Expansion**
1989–1993
New Haven, Connecticut
Yale University

Peachtree Triangle
1989
Atlanta, Georgia
Bramalea USA Urban Properties Inc.
Project

**Bushnell Theater Addition
Feasibility Study**
1989
Hartford, Connecticut
Bushnell Theater

***New North Terminal,
Washington National Airport**
1990–1996
Washington, DC
Metropolitan Washington Airports
Authority

School of Music Library
1990
New Haven, Connecticut
Yale University

**Investment Building Renovation
and Expansion**
1990
Washington, DC
The Kaempfer Company
Project

Comerica Headquarters Building
1990
Detroit, Michigan
Comerica Bank
Project

*NTT Shinjuku Headquarters Building
1990–1995
Tokyo, Japan
NTT International Inc.

*One Market
1991–1994
San Francisco, California
Yarmouth Group

1900 K Street
1991–1995
Washington, DC
The Kaempfer Company

*Ohio Center for the Arts—Cincinnati
1991–1995
Cincinnati, Ohio
Ohio Arts Facilities Commission;
Ohio Building Authority

***Humanities and Social Sciences
Building**
1991–1995
Riverside, California
University of California/Riverside

***Fukuoka Twin Dome City Master Plan;
Hakata Bay Oriental Hotel and Resort**
1991–1995
Fukuoka, Japan
Fukuoka Daiei Real Estate Inc.
Winning competition entry

**Uptown Boulevard Master Plan;
Uptown Hills Apartments**
1991–1993 (Phase I)
Houston, Texas
Interfin Corporation

Del Bosque
1991–1996
Mexico City, Mexico
Promociones Metropolis

*Kuala Lumpur City Centre, Phase I
1992–1996
Kuala Lumpur, Malaysia
Seri Kuda Sendirian Berhad
Winning competition entry

Bouchard Plaza
1992–1995
Buenos Aires, Argentina
Republica Propriedades S.A.

Radiation Effects Research Foundation
1992–1997
Hiroshima, Japan
Radiation Effects Research Foundation

Wachovia Corporate Headquarters
1992–1995
Winston-Salem, North Carolina
Wachovia Bank
Winning competition entry

Lutheran General Hospital Expansion
1992–1995
Park Ridge, Illinois
Lutheran General Hospital

**Middle and North Parking Structure,
Washington National Airport**
1992–1996
Washington, DC
Metropolitan Washington Airports
Authority

**Cleveland Clinic Foundation Health
Sciences Center**
1993–1995
Cleveland, Ohio
Cleveland Clinic Foundation

**Texas Heart Institute at St Luke's
Episcopal Hospital**
1993–1996
Houston, Texas
St Luke's Episcopal Hospital

Jeraisy Business Center
1993–1996
Riyadh, Saudi Arabia
Al-Jeraisy
Winning competition entry

**Pan American Health
Organization Headquarters**
1993–1997
Chevy Chase, Maryland
Pan American Health Organization
Winning competition entry

Awards and Exhibitions

Awards

Merit Finalist, Benedictus Award Competition
AIA/ACSA Council on Architectural Research, the International Union of Architects and the Du Pont Company
Founders Hall at NationsBank Corporate Center, Winter Garden at World Financial Center
1993

Excellence in Architecture Award
AIA New England
Carnegie Hall Tower
1993

Merit Award for University Building
International Masonry Institute/New Jersey Masonry Center
Institute for Advanced Study
1993

Design of the Year Award
Services for Independent Living
Cleveland Marriott Hotel at Society Center
1992

Award, Architecture
Los Angeles Beautiful Inc.
Plaza Tower
1992

Bard Award
The City Club of New York
Winter Garden at World Financial Center
1992

Special Citation
The City Club of New York
Carnegie Hall Tower
1992

Commendation, Structural Steel Design Awards Scheme
The British Constructional Steelwork Association Limited
Canary Wharf Tower
1992

Award of Merit
Chicago Lighting Institute
181 West Madison
1992

Design of the Year Award
Services for Independent Living
Cleveland Marriott Society Center
1992

Award, Architecture
Los Angeles Beautiful Inc.
Plaza Tower
1992

Bard Award
The City Club of New York
Winter Garden at World Financial Center
1992

Special Citation
The City Club of New York
Carnegie Hall Tower
1992

Commendation, Structural Steel Design Awards Scheme
The British Constructional Steelwork Association Limited
Canary Wharf Tower
1992

Award of Merit
Chicago Lighting Institute
181 West Madison
1992

Award of Merit
Illuminating Engineering Society of North America
Plaza Tower
1992

Design for Excellence/Certificate of Merit
Southern California Edison
Plaza Tower
1991

Honor Award
Orange County Chapter of the American Institute of Architects
Plaza Tower
1991

Design Award
Connecticut Society of Architects/American Institute of Architects
Boyer Center for Molecular Medicine
1991

Design Award
Connecticut Society of Architects/American Institute of Architects
Carnegie Hall Tower
1991

First Place Winner
Masonry Institute of New York City and Long Island
Carnegie Hall Tower
1991

Design Award
Modern Healthcare/American Institute of Architects
St Luke's Medical Tower
1991

Award of Excellence
American Institute of Steel Construction Inc.
Pacific Design Center Expansion
1990

Merit Award
Connecticut Society of Architects/American
Institute of Architects
Pacific Design Center Expansion
1990

Unbuilt Projects Award
Connecticut Society of Architects/American
Institute of Architects
Miglin-Beitler Tower
1990

Design 100 Editorial Award
Metropolitan Review Magazine
Yerba Buena Tower
April 1990

Firm Award
American Institute of Architects
1989

Brick in Architecture Award
Brick Institute of America
Herring Hall, Rice University
1989

**Building of the Year Award
(under 100,000 square feet)**
Connecticut Building Owners
and Managers Association
Century Executive Park Master
Plan and Office Building
1989

Domino's Top 30 Architects
1989

Excellence in Masonry Award
Masonry Institute of Connecticut
Century Executive Park Master Plan
and Office Building
1989

Award
Minnesota Chapter of the National
Association of Industrial and Office Parks
Norwest Center
1989

**Award for Excellence for the Outstanding
Large Scale Office Building**
Urban Land Institute
Norwest Center
1989

Award
Connecticut Commission on the Arts
1988

Unbuilt Project Award
Connecticut Society of Architects/American
Institute of Architects
Columbus Circle
1988

Domino's Top 30 Architects
1988

**Interiorscape Magazine Award
Best Project, Grand Winner**
World Financial Center Winter Garden
March/April 1988

Excellence in Design Award
New York State Society of Architects
Museum of Modern Art Gallery
Expansion and Residential Tower
1988

**Outstanding Achievement Award in
Architecture**
Port Authority Hispanic Society
1988

Beautification Award, Landmark Award
West Los Angeles Chamber of Commerce
Pacific Design Center Expansion
1988

Design Award
Connecticut Society of Architects/American
Institute of Architects
Ley Student Center, Rice University
1987

National Academy of Design Associate
1987

Design Award
Progressive Architecture
Pacific Design Center Expansion
1987

**U.N. Frederico Villarreal Le Corbusier
Plaque**
1987

Honor Award
American Institute of Architects
Cleveland Clinic
1986

Honor Award
American Institute of Architects
Herring Hall, Rice University
1986

Chicago Award
Illinois Council of the American Institute
of Architects/Architectural Record
1986

Outstanding Architect
Minnesota Real Estate Journal Award
1986

Design Award
Connecticut Society of Architects/American
Institute of Architects
Herring Hall, Rice University
1985

Award
Industrial Design Society of America
1985

Certificate of Merit
The Municipal Art Society of New York
World Financial Center
1985

Award
Urban Land Institute
Museum of Modern Art Gallery
Expansion and Residential Tower
1985

Certificate
American Society of Interior Designers
1984

Restoration and Expansion Award
Building Owners and Managers Association
of Greater New York Inc.
Museum of Modern Art Gallery Expansion
and Residential Tower
1984

Certificate of Commendation
City of Los Angeles
1984

Arnold W. Brunner Memorial Prize
American Academy/Institute of Arts and
Letters
1978

Citation
Progressive Architecture
Rainbow Center Mall and Winter Garden
1977

Citation
Southern California Chapter of the
American Institute of Architects
Fox Hills Mall
1976

Honor Award
Southern California Chapter of the
American Institute of Architects
Pacific Design Center
1976

Honor Award
Southern California Chapter of the
American Institute of Architects
Federal Office Building
1975

Honor Award
Southern California Chapter of the
American Institute of Architects
San Bernardino City Hall
1975

Merit Award
Southern California Chapter of the
American Institute of Architects
The Commons and Courthouse Center
1975

Merit Award
Southern California Chapter of the
American Institute of Architects
Wells Fargo Building
1975

**William E. Lehman Award for Architectural
Excellence**
Western Electric Building
1974

Merit Award
Bay Area Chapter of the American Institute
of Architects
Wells Fargo Building
1974

First Prize
International Architectural Competition
UN City, Vienna, Austria
1969

Honor Award
Southern California Chapter of the
American Institute of Architects
Worldway Postal Center
1969

Merit Award
Southern California Chapter of the
American Institute of Architects
Third Street Tunnel Extension
1969

Honor Award
American Institute of Steel Construction
Teledyne Systems Laboratories
1968

Citation
Progressive Architecture
Comsat Laboratories
1967

First Design Award
Progressive Architecture
Urban Nucleus, Sunset Mountain Park
1966

Exhibitions

Cesar Pelli: Architecture of Response
Delphi Research Inc., Tokyo, Japan
1994

American Skyscrapers
Findlandia Hall, League of Finnish–
American Societies/Finnish–American
Cultural Institute, Helsinki, Finland
1993

1992 Century Architects' Show
Kansai Airport
The Century Association, New York
April–May 1992

A Casa Latino–Americana/The Latin American House Exposition
Long Gallery House
CEAU (Centro de Estudos Arquitetoticos-
Urbanisticos), Rio de Janeiro, Brazil
January–March 1992

Architecture and Cities in the Age of the Global Environment
Osaka Association of Architects & Building
Engineers
May 1992

Retrospective on Cesar Pelli
College of Architecture Gallery,
University of North Carolina, Charlotte
September–November 1992

Rice Campus Buildings
Herring Hall and Ley Student Center
Farish Gallery, Rice University School of
Architecture, Houston, Texas
October–December 1991

Academic Buildings
Mathematics, Computing
and Engineering Center
School of Architecture, Roger Williams
College, Bristol, Rhode Island
September–November 1991

Cesar Pelli Architect
Frances Lehman Loeb Art Center, Vassar
College, Poughkeepsie, New York
June 1991

The Art of Architectural Drawings and Photography in America, 1959–1990
World Financial Center and Carnegie
Hall Tower
The Rye Arts Center, Rye, New York
April–June 1991

Cesar Pelli's Architecture: Process and Product
The Lamont Gallery, Phillips Exeter
Academy, Exeter, New Hampshire
February–March 1991

6 Studios of the American East Coast
Centro Cueltural, Buenos Aires, Argentina
July–September 1990

Cesar Pelli Retrospective
Brooks Hall Rotunda, School of Design,
North Carolina State University, Raleigh
October–November 1991

The Panorama of New York City
Carnegie Hall Tower Model
The Queens Museum, Flushing
Meadows, Corona Park, New York
June 1990

New Chicago Projects
181 West Madison and Miglin-Beitler Tower
The Chicago Athenaeum: Center for
Architecture, Art and Urban Studies,
Chicago, Illinois
October–December 1989

Architects' Drawings from the Barbara Pine Collection
Wight Art Gallery, University of California,
Los Angeles
October–November 1989

Connotations: Architects, Designers and Planners for Social Responsibility
Murray Feldman Gallery, West Hollywood,
California
October 1989

Tall Buildings
World Financial Center, Norwest Tower,
and Miglin-Beitler Tower
Perth, Australia
October 1989

Biennale of Architecture
181 W. Madison and Miglin-Beitler Tower
Buenos Aires, Argentina
September 1989

New York: 1970–1990
Deutsches Architekturmuseum, Frankfurt,
Germany
June–August 1989

Interarch '89 – World Biennale of Architecture
International Academy of Architecture and
the Union of Architects of Bulgaria, Sofia
Bulgaria
June 1989

What Could Have Been: Unbuilt Architecture of the 1980s
Columbus Circle
Cooper-Hewitt Museum, New York
July–October 1988

California Lifeguard Towers
Kirsten Kiser Gallery for Architecture,
Los Angeles
June–August 1988

Connecticut Arts Awards
Connecticut Commission on the Arts,
Choate Rosemary Hall, Wallingford,
Connecticut
June 1988

Architectural Art: Affirming the Relationship
American Craft Museum, New York
May–September 1988

1988: The World of Art Today
Museum of Modern Art Gallery Expansion
and Residential Tower
Milwaukee Art Museum, Milwaukee,
Wisconsin
May–August 1988

10 on 10
World Financial Center and Museum of
Modern Art Gallery Expansion and
Residential Tower
AIA New York, American Institute of
Architects National Convention, New York
May 1988

L.A. Architecture: 12 + 12 An Overview
American Institute of Architects Los Angeles
Chapter, West Hollywood, California
March 1988

Monumental Arches: Arches for Galveston
Cooper-Hewitt Museum, New York
October 1987–January 1988

**Yale University School of Architecture
Faculty Show**
Boyer Center for Molecular Medicine,
New Haven, Connecticut
October 1987

New New York
The Queens Museum, Flushing Meadows,
Corona Park, New York
July–September 1987

Recollections: A Decade of Collecting
Indiana Tower
Cooper-Hewitt Museum, New York
March 1987

Texas Architecture: The State of the Art
Herring Hall and Ley Student Center
Archer H. Huntington Art Gallery and
the Center for the Study of American
Architecture, The University of Texas
at Austin
March 1987

7ieux? de travail
World Financial Center
Centre Georges Pompidou, Centre de
Création Industrielle CCI, Paris, France
June–October 1986

**Silent Auction: Architects, Designers and
Planners for Social Responsibility**
Norwest Center skybridge
Max Protetch Gallery, New York
June 1986

Cesar Pelli: Current Work
Schindler House Gallery, Los Angeles
March–May 1986

Modern Redux
Herring Hall
Grey Art Gallery and Study Center,
New York University Art Collection,
New York, New York
February–April 1986

The Future of the Metropolises
World Financial Center
Technische Universität, Berlin,
West Germany
October–November 1985

**Artists and Architects: Challenges in
Collaboration**
World Financial Center and World
Financial Center Plaza
Cleveland Center for Contemporary Art,
Cleveland, Ohio
October–November 1985

Der Spirale
Indiana Tower
Art and Trade Museum, Basel, Switzerland
June 1985

**Silent Auction: Architects, Designers
and Planners for Social Responsibility**
Max Protetch Gallery, New York
May 1985

Design Histories
Herring Hall
University of Maryland School of
Architecture
February–March 1985

**The First Triennial of World Architecture/
Fifty Outstanding Architects of the World**
Belgrade, Yugoslavia
February 1985

Sites and Solutions: Recent Public Art
World Financial Center and World
Financial Center Plaza
Freedman Art Gallery, Albright College
Reading, Pennsylvania
October–November 1984

Aesthetics of Progress
Museum of Modern Art Gallery
Expansion and Residential Tower
and Four Leaf Towers
MIT Haydn Gallery, Cambridge,
Massachusettes
June 1984

Olympic Architects '84/84
Pacific Design Center Phases I, II, III, World
Financial Center and World Financial
Centre Plaza, Four Leaf Towers, Four Oaks
Towers, and Museum of Modern Art
Gallery Expansion and Residential Tower
American Institute of Architects National
Convention, West Hollywood, California
May 1984

Drawings of Works in Progress
Humana Office Building
Form and Function Gallery,
Atlanta, Georgia
April–June 1983

Trends in Contemporary Architecture
National Gallery, Athens, Greece
December 1982–January 1983

**Architecture on Paper: American and
European Drawings from New York State
Collections**
Museum of Modern Art Gallery Expansion
and Residential Tower
Tyler Fine Arts Gallery, State University of
New York at Oswego
September–October 1982

New American Art Museums
Museum of Modern Art Gallery Expansion
and Residential Tower
Whitney Museum of American Art,
New York
June–October 1982

**Work by Newly Elected Members and
Recipients of Honors and Awards**
World Financial Center and Four Oaks
Towers
American Academy and Institute of Arts
and Letters Art Gallery and Museum
New York, New York
May–June 1982

Homage to de Stijl
Museum of Modern Art Gallery Expansion
and Residential Tower
Walker Art Center, Minneapolis, Minnesota
January–March 1982

16/19
Untitled Sketches
Otis Art Institute of Parson's School
of Design Art Auction, New York
January 1982

Build Art/Build Arts–of the Arts Edge
Museum of Modern Art Gallery Expansion
and Residential Tower
US Steel Building, Pittsburgh, Pennsylvania
October 1981

Architecture in Houston since 1945
Four Leaf Towers and Hermann
Park Towers
Rice School of Architecture and Rice
Design Alliance, Houston, Texas
September–October 1981

Creation and Recreation: America Draws
Museum of Norwegian Architecture, May
1981; Museum of Modern Art,
Copenhagen
August–September 1981

Collaboration: Artists and Architects
Hexagonal Room
Centennial Exhibition of the Architectural
League of New York, New York Historical
Society
March–June 1981

Architecture II: Houses for Sale
Long Gallery House
Leo Castelli Gallery, New York
October 1980

City Segments
Museum of Modern Art Gallery Expansion
and Residential Tower
Walker Art Center, Minneapolis, Minnesota
April–June 1980

Trends in Contemporary Architecture
Columbus Commons and Courthouse
Center
The New Gallery of Contemporary Art,
Cleveland, Ohio
October–November 1978

**Work by Newly Elected Members and
Recipients of Honors and Awards**
Pacific Design Center, Columbus Commons
and Courthouse Center, US Embassy
(Tokyo), UN City (Vienna), and San
Bernardino (CA) City Hall
American Academy and Institute of Arts and
Letters, Art Gallery and Museum, New York
May 1978

**A View of California Architecture
1960–1976**
San Francisco Museum of Art
December 1976–February 1977

Suburban Alternatives
Biennale House
Venice Biennale
Venice, Italy
July 1976

The Los Angeles 12
Pacific Design Center
California Polytechnic–Pomona,
Architecture Department
May 1976

Bibliography

Abercrombie, Stanley. "MOMA Builds Again." *Architecture* (October 1984): pp. 87–95.

Abercrombie, Stanley. "Waterfront Delights and the Price of Progress." *AIA Journal* (June 1982): pp. 30–35.

"Admiring Canary Wharf's Stone Plumage." *Stone World* (March 1993): pp. 35–36.

Affleck, Raymond T., et al. "24th Annual Awards: Rainbow Center." *Progressive Architecture* (January 1977): p. 65.

Ai Dingzheng and Li Shu (eds). *Cesar Pelli.* Famous Foreign Architect Series, Number 2. (Beijing: 1991).

"Aluminum Membrane Envelops Satellite Laboratory." *Architectural and Engineering News* (November 1968).

Amaya, Mario. "The New MOMA: A 'Machine for Looking.'" *Studio International* special edition (London, 1984) : pp. 54–55.

American Architecture of the 1980's. Washington, DC: The American Institute of Architects Press, 1990, pp. 162–169, 218–225.

"And Then There Were Twelve: The Los Angeles 12." *Architectural Record* (August 1976): p. 90.

Anderson, Grace. "MOMA." *Architectural Record* (March 1981): pp. 94–99.

Anderson, Lawrence, et al. "Progressive Architecture Design Awards 1968: Comsat Laboratories." *Progressive Architecture* (January 1968): pp. 121–125.

Archer, B.J., et al. Review of "Houses for Sale" exhibition. *A + U* (December 1980): pp. 81–112.

Arnell, Peter and Ted Bickford (eds). *A Center for the Visual Arts: The Ohio State University Competition.* New York: Rizzoli International Publications, 1984, pp. 33–51.

Arnell, Peter, et al. *A Tower for Louisville: The Humana Competition.* New York: Rizzoli International Publications, 1982, pp. 69–86.

"Balancing the Equation." *Architectural Record* (November 1991): pp. 102–109.

Barnett, Jonathan. "In the Public Interest: Design Guidelines." *Architectural Record* (July 1987): pp. 114–125.

Barrick, Adrian. "New Challenger in Sky Wars: Architects: Cesar Pelli & Associates." *Building Design* (London, June 2, 1989): p. 3.

Battisti, Eugenio, et al. "School and Society." *l'Arca* (Milan, June 1988): pp. 46–51.

"Big Rock Sunset Mountain: Urban Nucleus." *Architectural Review* (June 1966): pp. 414–415.

Bill, Peter and Martin Spring. "Canary Wharf." *Building* (April 1, 1988): pp. 8–9.

"Blue Danube Prize: International Congress Center in Vienna." *The Architectural Forum* (November 1969): pp. 31–32.

Boles, Daralice Donkervoet. "Made in Minneapolis." *Progressive Architecture* (March 1989): pp. 74–81.

Boles, Daralice Donkervoet. "MOMA's Back in Town." *Progressive Architecture* (September 1984): pp. 27–28.

Boles, Daralice Donkervoet. "Practicing What He Preaches." *Progressive Architecture* (March 1989): p. 73.

Bottero, Maria. "The Architectural Querelle: Design in the United States Today." *Abitare* (Milan, April 1984): pp. 90–95.

Branch, Mark Alden. "Cesar Pelli." *Art New England* (April 1990) pp. 11–13.

Brandt, Anthony. "The Way to Go." *Connoisseur* (November 1982): pp. 124–129.

Brenner, Douglas. "New Layers of Meaning: Works in Progress by Cesar Pelli." *Architectural Record* (July 1983): pp. 104–113.

"Buildings in Context." *Center* (vol. 1, 1985) : pp. 124–135.

Burns, James T. "Jewel of a Setting: Interior for a Jewelers Center in Beverly Hills." *Progressive Architecture* (February 1967): pp. 150–153 .

"Centre Commercial et Municipal, Columbus, Indiana." *l' Architecture d'Aujourd'hui* (Paris, October 1977): pp. 36–40.

"Centro medico a Houston." *l'Industria Delle Costruzioni* (Rome, October 1992): pp. 28–33.

"Centro Ideale Presso Santa Monica." *Architettura: Cronache e Storia* (Rome, January 1968): pp. 600–601.

"Cesar Pelli." *Architectural Design* (London, no. 3/4, 1981): pp. 36–37.

"Cesar Pelli: Architectural Design which Serves the City." *A T* (July 1990): pp. 7–30.

Cesar Pelli Buildings and Projects 1965–1990. New York: Rizzoli International Publications, 1990.

"Cesar Pelli—Carnegie Hall Tower." *A + U* (April 1992): pp. 110–117.

"Cesar Pelli." *Designers West* (December 1968): p. 23.

"Cesar Pelli Given State Arts Award." *CSA/AIA News* (September 1988): p. 3.

"Cesar Pelli: Hermann Park Towers, Houston, Texas." *Architectural Design* (London, no. 3/4, 1981): pp. 36–37.

"Cesar Pelli Named Dean of the Yale School of Architecture." *Interiors* (September 1976): p. 4.

"Cesar Pelli Talks About the Past, Present and Promise of Architecture and Interiors." *Interior Design* (April 1982): pp. 224–226.

"Cesar Pelli & Associates Voted Most Outstanding Firm of 1989." *A + U* (March 1989): p. 3.

"Cesar Pelli & Associates — World Financial Center, New York City." *A + U* (Tokyo, no. 4 supplement, April 1988): pp. 48–63.

"Cesar Pelli's Winning Design for 'Commercial Core' of Battery Park City." *Architectural Record* (July 1981): p. 41.

Chang, Ching-yu. "Phenomenal Architecture: Cesar Pelli." *Process: Architecture* (Tokyo, July 1979).

"Collegial Crosstalk." *Architectural Record* (November 1992): pp. 68–73.

"Comsat Laboratories." *Architectural Review* (Westminster, England, November 1969): p. 343.

Constantopoulos, Elias. "Modern Greek Dramas." *Building Design* (London, January 28, 1983): pp. 18–19.

"Consultazione Internazionale Fiat Lingotto: Cesar Pelli." *Architettura: Cronache e Storia* (Rome, May 1984): p. 372.

"Conversation: Cesar Pelli on Architectural Technology." *Architectural Design* (London, mid-August 1979): pp. 66–67.

Daix, Pierre. "Deux des Nouveaux Museés: la Renovation du Museum of Modern Art et la Nouvelle Aile de la National Gallery." *Gazette des Beaux Arts* (Paris, September 1984): pp. 1–3.

"Dalla California Progetti e Opere di Cesar Pelli." *Domus* (Milan, November 1968): pp. 12–18.

Davis, Douglas. "Designs for Living." *Newsweek* (November 6, 1978): pp. 82–91.

Davis, Douglas. "MOMA Lets the Sunshine In." *Newsweek* (May 21, 1984): p. 88.

Davis, Douglas. "The New Master Builder: Pelli's Lyrical Designs Please On Many Levels." *Newsweek* (August 4, 1986): p. 61.

Davis, Douglas, with Maggie Malone. "The Sky's the Limit." *Newsweek* (November 8, 1982): pp. 66–76.

Dean, Andrea Oppenheimer and Allan Freeman. "The Rockefeller Center of the '80's?: Battery Park City's Core." *Architecture* (December 1986): pp. 36–43.

Dean, Andrea Oppenheimer. "Speaking Softly and in Strong Colors: Four Leaf Condominium Towers, Houston." *AIA Journal* (May 1983): pp. 168–173.

Dechau, Wilfried. "New Life for A Fossil: Suggested New Uses for the Closed Fiat-Lingotto Car Factory in Turin." *Deutsches Bauzeitung* (Stuttgart, June 1984): pp. 63–74.

"Design Report NTT Shinjuku Building: Pelli Realizes High Tech Company's Image Followed Up by Yamashita." *Nikkei Architecture* (Tokyo, February 1993): pp. 192–197.

Diamonstein, Barbaralee (ed). *American Architecture Now.* New York: Rizzoli International Publications, 1980: pp. 163–182.

Diamonstein, Barbaralee, et al. *Collaboration: Artists and Architects exhibition catalogue.* New York Historical Society, March 5–June 7, 1981. New York: Whitney Library of Design, 1981, pp. 118–125.

Dillon, David. "Herring Hall, Combining Adventure and Respect: Rice University." *Architecture* (May 1985): pp.174–181.

Dixon, John Morris. "Green Phase." *Progressive Architecture* (March 1989): pp. 82–85.

Dixon, John Morris. "Piazza, American Style: Courthouse Center and the Commons, Columbus, Indiana." *Progressive Architecture* (June 1976): pp. 64–69.

Duncan, Carol and Alan Wallach. "MOMA: Ordeal and Triumph on Fifty-third Street." *Studio International* (London, January 1987): pp. 48–57.

Dunster, David. "Cesar Pelli Arrives in Houston." *Skyline* (March 1983): pp. 16–19.

"The Eero Saarinen Spawn." *Inland Architect* (May 1981): pp.14–44.

Ellis, William S. "Skyscrapers." *National Geographic* (February 1989): pp. 143–173.

"Extra Edition: Cesar Pelli." *A + U* (July 1985).

Filler, Martin. "High Ruse." *Art in America* (October 1984): pp.170–171.

"Final Design Unveiled for Minneapolis Tower." *Architectural Record* (October 1986): p. 57.

"Four Days in May: White, Silver and Grey Conference." *A + U* (Tokyo, September 1974): pp. 15–19.

"Four Leaf Towers and Four Oaks." *GA Document* (Tokyo, no. 12, January 1985): pp. 108–140.

"Four Leaf Towers, Houston, Texas." *Architectural Record* (June 1980): p. 41.

"Fox Hills Mall." *A + U* (February 1973): pp. 52–53.

Fox, Stephen. "Enlightened Hindsight: Pelli's Herring Hall." *Arts & Architecture* (July 1985): pp. 78–83.

Frampton, Kenneth. "Cesar Pelli/Gruen Associates." *GA 59* (Tokyo, 1981).

Frampton, Kenneth, "Cesar Pelli: San Bernardino City Hall, California." *Architectural Design* (London, July/August 1982): pp. 114–119.

Gebhard, David and Susan King. *A View of California Architecture: 1960–1976.* Exhibition catalogue. San Francisco Museum of Modern Art: December 18, 1976–February 6, 1977, pp. 20–21.

Goldberger, Paul. "A Meeting of Artistic Minds." Review of "Collaboration: Artists and Architects" exhibition. *New York Times Magazine* (March 1, 1981): pp.70–73.

Goldberger, Paul. "A Yankee Upstart Sprouts in Thatcher's London." *New York Times* (November 26, 1989): p. 37.

Goldberger, Paul. "Battery Park City Is a Triumph Of Urban Design." *New York Times* (August 31, 1986): sec. II, pp. 1, 28.

Goldberger, Paul. "Boston's Chance for its Own Battery Park City." *New York Times* (June 28, 1987): pp.11, 23.

Goldberger, Paul. "Carnegie Hall Unveils Plans for Office Tower." *New York Times* (April 30,1986): sec. III, p. 19.

Goldberger, Paul. "Cesar Pelli Seeks the Perfect Skyscraper." *New York Times* (January 15, 1989): p. 30.

Goldberger, Paul. "Dramatic Counterpoint to the World Trade Center." *New York Times* (May 24,1981) sec. II: p.5.

Goldberger, Paul. "Glass Building on Coast Stirs Dispute." *New York Times* (September 2, 1975): p. 36.

Goldberger, Paul. "Houston Architecture Typifies 'Changing Attitude.'" *New York Times* (October 10, 1981): p. 8.

Goldberger, Paul. "The New American Skyscraper." *New York Times Magazine* (November 8, 1981): pp. 68–93.

Goldberger, Paul. "The New MOMA." *New York Times Magazine* (April 15, 1984): pp. 36–49, 68–71.

Goldberger, Paul. *The Skyscraper.* New York: Alfred A. Knopf, 1982, pp. 147, 149, 158–160, 163.

Goldberger, Paul. "Wintergarden at Battery Park City." *New York Times* (October 12, 1988): C15.

Good, R. Lawrence. "Color in Texas Architecture." *Texas Architect* (May/June 1981): pp. 60–65.

Gray, Lee Edward and David Walters. *Pattern and Context: Essays on Cesar Pelli.* Charlotte, NC: 1992.

Grenon, Nathalie. "On the Hudson at Battery Park City." *l'Arca* (Milan, July/August 1987): pp. 58–65.

"Harmonious Neighbor." *Architecture* (June 1991): pp. 97–101.

"Hermann Towers, Houston, Texas." *GA Document* (Tokyo, no. 1, Summer 1980): pp. 76–77.

"Herring Hall, Rice University, Houston." *Baumeister* (Munich, November 1985): pp. 22–26.

Herron, R. "Something Borrowed, Something Blue: Pacific Design Center in Los Angeles." *RIBA Journal* (London, March 1977): pp. 95–96.

Hewitt, M.A. "Two Campuses: Lessons from Rice and University of Houston." *Texas Architect* (September/October 1984): pp. 66–72.

"Highly Refined." *Architectural Record* (August 1991): pp. 100–107.

"High-Wired Act." *Architectural Record* (June 1992): pp. 82–84.

"Hôtel de Ville San Bernardino." *l'Architecture d'Aujourd'hui* (Paris, July 1973): pp. 68–69.

Hughes, Robert. "Revelation on 53rd Street." *Time* (May 14, 1984): pp. 78–80.

Hughes, Robert. "US Architects: Doing Their Own Thing." *Time* (January 8, 1979): pp. 52–59.

"Humana Headquarters Design Competition." *Architectural Record* (July 1982): pp. 58–59.

Huxtable, Ada Louise. "A New Rockefeller Center Planned for Battery Park." *New York Times* (May 24, 1981) sec II: p. 25.

Huxtable, Ada Louise. "The Modern Prepares for Expansion." *New York Times* (June 29, 1980): D1, D26.

Huxtable, Ada Louis. *The Tall Building Artistically Reconsidered: The Search for a Skyscraper Style.* New York: Pantheon Books, 1984, pp. 57, 61, 85–87.

"Interview: Cesar Pelli and Peter Eisenman." *Skyline* (May 1982): pp. 22–25.

"An Interview with Cesar Pelli." *Cite* (August 1982).

Irace, Fulvio. "A Question of Skin." *Ottagono* (Milan, June 1986): pp. 60–65.

Irace, Fulvio. "New York Strikes Again." *Domus* (Milan, February 1983): pp. 2–10.

Ito, Tadahiko. "The Third Generation Architect & Concept." *Hakuba Shuppan, Inc.* (Tokyo, July 1974): pp. 15–65.

Jackson, Paul Rice. "The Pacific Design Center Breaks New Ground for its $150-million-dollar Expansion." *Interiors* (February 1987): pp. 61–65.

Johnson, Robert. "Sometimes Being the Tallest Isn't Quite Tall Enough." *Wall Street Journal* (New York, July 7, 1989): p. 1.

"Kansai International Airport: Cesar Pelli." *Architectural Design* (London, no. 3/4 1989): pp. 55–58.

"Kansai International Airport Competition." *Nikkei Architecture* (Tokyo, January 23,1989): pp. 196–227.

Karson, Robin. "Battery Park City: Winter Garden." *Landscape Architecture* (January/February 1986): pp. 76–77.

Kay, Jane Holtz. "New Design for Boston Fan Piers." *Progressive Architecture* (April 1987): pp. 35–36.

Kruger, Karl Heinz. "Ein Glücksfall, nicht nur fur America." *Der Spiegel* (Hamburg, October 20, 1986): pp. 256–264.

Kudalis, Eric. "From the Ashes." *Architecture Minnesota* (March/April 1989): pp. 22–27.

"La NTT di Tokyo." *l'Arca* (Rome, January 1993): pp. 62–72.

"Laboratori in Campagna." *Domus* (Milan, March 1971): pp. 6–10.

Larson, Kay. "MOMA Unveils its Treasures." *New York* (May 14, 1984): pp. 34–49.

Leers, Andrea. "Contemporary Student Spirit: Japan–America interview with Professor Kazuo Shinohara and with Cesar Pelli." *Japan Architect* (Tokyo, July 1985): pp. 44–47.

Lucain, Pierre. "Les Nouveaux Gratte-Ciels Americains: La Cinquième Géneration." *l'Architecture d'Aujourd'hui* (Paris, no. 220, April 1982): pp. 86–87.

Macmillan Encyclopedia of Architects, Adolf K. Placzek, ed. London: Collier Macmillan Publishers, 1982.

Macrae-Gibson, Gavin. "Four Leaf Towers: Icons of the Non-Ideal." *A + U* (Tokyo, February 1983): pp. 19–30.

Macrae-Gibson, Gavin. *The Secret Life of Buildings: An American Mythology for Modern Architecture.* London and Cambridge, Mass.: MIT Press, 1985, pp. 52–73.

Macrae-Gibson, Gavin and Lynne Breslin. "The Museum of Modern Art." *A + U* (December 1984): pp. 31–66.

Maldonado, Tomás et al. "Sul Futuro dell' Architettura: Riposte a un Questionario." *Casabella* (Milan, November/December 1981): p. 98.

McCoy, Esther. "Before the Silvers." *Progressive Architecture* (October 1976): pp. 66–69.

McCoy, Esther. "The Blue Bombshell." *Progressive Architecture* (October 1976): pp. 78–83.

McCoy, Esther. "High-Tech Images." *Progressive Architecture* (February 1974): pp. 66–71.

McCoy, Esther. "Planned for Change: Cesar Pelli Designs an Adaptable Electronics Plant." *The Architectural Forum* (July/August 1968): pp. 102–107.

McCoy, Esther. *The Second Generation.* Salt Lake City: Peregrine Books, 1984, pp. xi–xv.

"Modernidad y Tradición, de sur a norte." *Summa* (April 1991): pp. 24–38.

Moholy-Nagy, Sibyl. "Cesar Pelli: Public Architect." *The Architectural Forum* (March 1970): pp. 42–47.

Moiraghi, Luigi. "Canary Wharf in London." *l'Arca* (Milan, January 1990): pp. 14–27.

Moiraghi, Luigi. "Norwest Center." *l'Arca* (July/August 1989): pp. 28–33.

Moiraghi, Luigi. "Ultima Frontiera." *Domus* (June 1985): pp. 12–27.

"MOMA Extension, New York." *Werk, Bauen und Wohnen* (Zurich, January/February 1985): pp. 15–17.

"The MOMA Gallery Expansion and Residential Tower, New York." *Architectural Design* (London, no. 1/2, 1985): pp. 36–37.

"MOMA: Extension to The Museum of Modern Art, New York." *Baumeister* (Munich, August 1984): pp. 74–77.

"Monuments of nothingness? Zu neuen Arbeiten von Cesar Pelli." *Archithese* (Zurich, July/August 1980): pp. 19–24.

Moorhead, Gerald. "Galveston's Fantasy Arches: An Appreciation." *Texas Architect* (September/October 1986): pp. 50–56.

Morgan, Anne Lee and Colin Naylor (eds). *Contempory Architects.* London: St James Press, 1987.

Muchow, William, C., et al. "The 1978 AIA Honor Awards: U.S. Embassy in Tokyo." *AIA Journal* (May 1978): p. 148.

Murphy, Jim and Nory Miller. "Thinking Tall." *Progressive Architecture* (December 1980): pp. 45–57.

"Museum of Modern Art Extension, New York." *GA Document* (Tokyo, January 1985): pp. 29–42.

"The Museum of Modern Art: Gallery Expansion and Residential Tower." *A + U* (October 1980): pp. 110–114.

"Museum of Modern Art, New York." *GA Document* (Tokyo, no. 1, Summer 1980): pp. 78–80.

"Museum Tower and Enlargement of the MOMA in New York Project." *Casabella* (April/May 1980): pp. 44–48.

Nannerini, Giuseppe. "United States Embassy in Tokyo." *l' Industria Delle Costruzioni,* (Rome, April 1982): pp. 40–45.

"NCNB Center lifts Charlotte's Skyline." *Engineering News Record* (January 20, 1992): pp. 46–50.

"New Skyline Blooms at the foot of World Trade Center." *Nikkei Architecture* (July 1982): pp. 72–75.

"Noyau Urbain dans un Parc Regional en Californie." *l'Architecture d'Aujourd'hui* (June 1967): pp. 90–91.

Oculus. Special edition on the World Financial Center (vol. 46, no. 7, March 1985).

"Open Line City." *A + U* (Tokyo, March 1971): pp. 93–96.

"Open Line City." *Progressive Architecture* (June 1970): pp. 158–160.

"Pacific Design Center, Los Angeles." *l'Architecture d'Aujourd'hui* (Paris, October 1977): pp. 36–46.

Papademetriou, Peter and Craig Hodgetts. Interview with Cesar Pelli. *Design Quarterly* (no. 100, 1976): p. 25.

Papademetriou, Peter and Craig Hodgetts. "Pattern and Principle: Herring Hall, Rice University, Houston." *Progressive Architecture* (April 1985): pp. 86–97.

Papademetriou, Peter. "Pelli Crams Old and New into Rice's Future." *Cite* (Winter 1984): p. 84.

Papademetriou, Peter. "Rice Reprise." *Progressive Architecture* (February 1988): pp. 72–75.

Papademetriou, Peter. "The Silvers: Images from a Silver Screen." *Progressive Architecture* (October 1976): pp. 70–77.

Pastier, John. "Anchor for a Sprawling Medical Complex." *Architecture* (May 1986): pp. 210–213.

Pastier, John. *Cesar Pelli.* New York: Whitney Library of Design, 1980.

Pastier, John and Lance Knobel. "Cesar Pelli." *Architectural Review* (London, March 1981): pp. 191–192.

Pastier, John. "Evaluation: Utility and Fantasy in Los Angeles." *AIA Journal* (May 1978): pp. 38–45.

Pastier, John. "A Monument Becomes an Ensemble." *Architecture* (June 1989): pp. 108–111.

Pastier, John. "The Pacific Design Center: A Blue Whale Borne Upon the Shifting Comments of Modern Architecture." *Decade* (May 1979): pp. 52–60.

Pastier, John. "The Sophisticated Skins of Cesar Pelli." *AIA Journal* (December 1981): pp. 74–85.

Patton, Phil. "Manhattan's World Financial Center." *Diversion* (July 1989): pp. 157–169.

"Pelle e/o ossa: la Cancelleria Dell'Ambasciata Americana a Tokyo." *Architettura: Cronache e Storia* (Rome, October 1977): pp. 318–319.

"Pelli al MOMA." *Architettura: Cronache e Storia* (Rome, June 1985): pp. 430–431.

"Pelli and Concrete Architecture — It Is Necessary to Develop the Modern Tradition." *Architettura: Cronache e Storia* (Rome, April 1983): p. 250.

"Pelli named Dean at Yale." *Progressive Architecture* (August 1976): pp. 19–20.

"Pelli Team Wins in Vienna." *Progressive Architecture* (November 1969): p. 40.

Pelli, Cesar (with Kikonori Kikutake). "A Documentary Exchange." *Japan Architect* (Tokyo, March 1977): pp. 29–36.

Pelli, Cesar. "Architects Working in Countries Other Than Their Own." *A + U* (Tokyo, January, 1993): p. 133.

Pelli, Cesar. "Architectural Form and the Tradition of Building." *A + U* (Tokyo, July 1985 extra edition): pp. 26–32.

Pelli, Cesar. "Architectural Form and the Tradition of Building," *via 7: The Journal of the University of Pennsylvania School of Architecture.* Cambridge: University of Pennsylvania and the MIT Press, 1985, pp. 145–160.

Pelli, Cesar (with Bernard Hanson). "Art and Architects: An Interview with Cesar Pelli." *State of the Arts,* published by the Connecticut Commission on the Arts (no. 14, Summer 1984): pp. 4–6.

Pelli, Cesar (with William Bailey). "Art and Architecture: The History and Future of Collaboration." *A + U* (Tokyo, May 1982): pp. 108–109.

Pelli, Cesar. "Biennale House Project." *A + U* (Tokyo, November 1976): pp. 109–116.

Pelli, Cesar. "Cesar Pelli & Associates: Canary Wharf Skyscraper." *Architectural Design* (London, no. 11/12, 1988): pp. 40–49.

Pelli, Cesar and Andreas Papadakis. "Cesar Pelli: The Mega-Building in Context." *Architectural Design* (London, November/ December 1988): pp. 50–53.

Pelli, Cesar. "The Challenge of the '90s." *Young Architects Forum.* Washington, DC: The American Institute of Architects, 1991: pp. 22–30.

Pelli, Cesar. *The Charlottesville Tapes* (introduction by Jaquelin Robertson). New York: Rizzoli International Publications, 1985: pp. 108–115.

Pelli, Cesar. *The Chicago Tapes* (introduction by Stanley Tigerman). New York: Rizzoli International Publications, 1987: pp. 204–215.

Pelli, Cesar. "Defining Paradigm." *Perspecta: The Yale Architectural Journal.* Cambridge: MIT Press, no. 22, 1986: pp. 100–101.

Pelli, Cesar (with Diana Balmori). "Eero Saarinen." *GA 6* (Tokyo, 1971): pp. 1–6.

Pelli, Cesar (with Diana Balmori). "Eero Saarinen." *A + U* (Tokyo, June 1979 extra edition): pp. 15–18.

Pelli, Cesar. "Excerpts from a Conversation." *Perspecta:The Yale Architectural Journal.* Cambridge: MIT Press, no. 19, 1983: pp. 127–137, 184–85.

Pelli, Cesar. "A Few Words on Philip Johnson's Buildings." *A + U* (Tokyo, May 1979 extra edition): p. 79.

Pelli, Cesar. "Four Buildings Responsive to their Critical Surroundings." *A + U* (Tokyo, January, 1993): pp. 104–105.

Pelli, Cesar. "The Glass Box: Pelli Explains Why." *Architectural and Engineering News* (November 1969): pp. 34–36.

Pelli, Cesar. "Joseph Paxton's Crystal Palace." *A + U* (Tokyo, February 1980): pp. 3–14.

Pelli, Cesar (with Diana Balmori). "Latin American Influence on US Architecture." *US Information Agency Bulletin* (March 1979).

Pelli, Cesar. "Nissan Motors Building." *A + U* (Tokyo, December 1972): pp. 15–27.

Pelli, Cesar. "Pieces of the City." *Architectural Digest* (August 1988): pp. 29–36.

Pelli, Cesar. "Skyscrapers." *Perspecta: The Yale Architectural Journal.* Cambridge: MIT Press, no. 18, 1982 : pp. 134–170.

Pelli, Cesar (with Paulhans Peters). "Skyscrapers in the USA." *Baumeister* (Berlin, February 1984): pp. 8–10, 17–24.

Pelli, Cesar. "Statement." *A + U* (Tokyo, February, 1990): p. 63–64.

Pelli, Cesar. "Thoughts about Louis I. Kahn." *A + U* (Tokyo, November 1983): p. 216.

Pelli, Cesar. "Thoughts on Supergraphics." *Approach* (Spring 1971): pp. 12–31, 38–39.

Pelli, Cesar. "Today & Tomorrow." *San Francisco Bay Architects' Review* (Spring 1983): pp. 12–15.

Pelli, Cesar. "Transparency—Physical and Perceptual" and "The Biennale House Project." *A + U* (Tokyo, November 1976): pp. 74–86.

Pelli, Cesar. "Worldway Postal Center, Los Angeles International Airport." *Lotus 6* (1969): 252–257.

Pelli, Cesar, (ed). *Yale Seminars on Architecture,* vol. 2, New Haven: Yale University, 1981: pp. 89–114.

Peters, Paulhans. "Fiat-Lingotto." *Baumeister* (Munich, May 1984): pp. 8–11.

Peters, Paulhans. "Wolkenkratzer and Stadt." *Baumeister* (Munich, February 1984): p. 47.

"P/A Sixteenth Annual Design Awards Program." *Progressive Architecture* (January 1969): p. 102–146.

"Rainbow Center Mall and Winter Garden." *A + U* (October 1978): pp. 41–48.

Ratcliff, Carter. "A Tour of the Modern." *Travel & Leisure* (January 1985): pp. 74–83, 104.

"Rediscovering the Skyscraper." *Blueprint* (November 1991): pp. 46–50.

Robinson, Cervin. "A Triumphal Arch, a Gateway and a Garden." *AIA Journal* (Mid-May 1979): pp. 114–117.

Robles, Eduardo. "The Galveston Arches: An Editorial." *Cite* (Summer 1986): p. 5.

Rosenbaum, Lee. "MOMA's Construction Project: Reflections on a Glass Tower." *Art in America* (November 1977): pp. 10–13.

Rosenfeld, M.N. "The New Museum of Modern Art, New York." *Vie des Arts* (Montreal, March 1985): pp. 30–33, 91.

Rub, Timothy F. "The Rise of Cesar Pelli's World Financial Center." *Manhattan, Inc.* (August 1985): pp. 125–128.

Sailer, John. *The Great Stone Architects.* Oradell, NJ: Tradelink Publishing Co., Inc., 1991: pp. 47–62.

Sakamoto, Wasaburo. "Architect at Work: Cesar Pelli." *A + U* (Tokyo, April 1983): p. 116.

"San Bernardino City Hall." *A + U* (Tokyo, December 1972): pp. 50–51.

Sands, Olivia. "Free Thinking Art and Functional Design on Show" Review of "Houses for Sale" exhibition. *Building Design* (London, November 14, 1980): pp. 30–31.

Sartogo, Piero. "Cesar Pelli Superstar." *Casabella* (Milan, October 1975): pp. 20–38.

Schmertz, Mildred. "The New MOMA: Modern Architecture for Modern Art." *Architectural Record* (October 1984): pp. 164–77.

Searing, Helen. *New American Art Museums.* Catalogue of exhibition at the Whitney Museum, New York. Berkeley: University of California Press, 1983: pp. 78–86.

Searing, Helen. *New American Art Museums.* Berkeley: The University of California in association with the Whitney Museum of Art, 1989.

"Security Pacific National Bank." *A + U* (Tokyo, April 1973): pp. 75–80.

Shapira, Nathan H. "The Extension of the Pacific Design Center." *Abitare 251* (Milan, January 1987): pp. 158–163.

"Showplace on the Prairie." *Time* (December 5, 1977): pp. 68–69.

Simpson, Jeffrey. "Two Cheers for MOMA." *ARTnews* (September 1984): pp. 56–61.

"Special Issue: Cesar Pelli." *A + U* (Tokyo, March 1971): pp. 14–100.

"Special Feature: Cesar Pelli." *A + U* (Tokyo, November 1976): pp. 27–120.

"Special Feature: The Recent Works of Cesar Pelli." *A + U* (Tokyo, February 1990): pp. 63–148.

Spring, Martin. "US Wins Main Canary Wharf Design; Gentle Giant at Canary Wharf." *Building* (October 30, 1987): pp. 8, 28–29.

Stephens, Suzanne. "Niagara Rises." *Progressive Architecture* (August 1978): pp. 72–81.

Stevens, Mark. "MOMA's Golden Anniversary." *Newsweek* (November 26, 1979): pp. 124–27.

Stucchi, Silvano. "Herring Hall, Rice University, Houston, Texas." *l'Industria Delle Costruzioni* (Rome, February 1986): pp. 34–41.

Stucchi, Silvano. "The World Financial Center in New York." *l' Industria Delle Costruzioni* (Rome, November 1988): pp. 38–49.

Strickland, Roy. "No Little Plans: An Ambitious Mixed-Use Scheme for Boston." *Architectural Record* (February 1987): pp. 60–61.

Suckle, Abby (ed). *By Their Own Design.* New York: Whitney Library of Design, 1980: pp. 18–29.

Sudjic, Deyan. "Niagara Halls." *Architectural Review* (London, March 1981): pp. 170–173.

Takase, Hayahiko. "A New Phase of Cesar Pelli." *Space Design* (Tokyo, September 1980): pp. 3–50.

"Tectonics: The Museum of Modern Art Tower." *Process: Architecture* (Tokyo, January 1986): pp. 46–49.

"Teledyne Laboratories." *Architectural Review* (London, November 1969): pp. 340–342.

"The Crown and the Curtain Wall." *Civil Engineering* (August 1992): pp. 62–65.

"Third Generation Architects." *A + U* (Tokyo, March 1971): pp. 18–22.

Tomkins, Calvin. "Agora." *The New Yorker* (October 15, 1984): pp. 12–33.

"Topics: Cesar Pelli & Associates." *Process: Architecture* (Tokyo, January 1986): pp. 72–77.

"Torre Un Siglo, Kuala Lumpur Centre." *Summa* (Buenos Aires, December 1992): pp. 18–22.

"Towering Urban Garden Under Glass." *Life* (December 1978): pp. 109–112.

Train, Kirk, David Spiker and Robert Jensen (eds). "The Museum of Modern Art Project." Interview with Cesar Pelli, Fred Clarke and Diana Balmori. *Perspecta: The Yale Architectural Journal.* Cambridge: MIT Press, no.16, 1980, pp. 96–107.

Tretiack, Philippe. "Lingotto." *Architecture Intérieure Creé* (Paris, May/June/July 1984): pp. 166–172.

12 Los Angeles Architects. Exhibition catalogue. Pomona: California State Polytechnic University, 1978: pp. 34–48.

"The Twenty-Third Awards Program: Architectural Design" and "Technics: Selected Details Inside the Looking Glass." *Progressive Architecture* (January 1976): pp. 55–93.

"The ULI Awards for Excellence." *Urban Land* (December 1984): pp. 22–23.

"United States Embassy, Tokyo." *Japan Architect* (Tokyo, November 1976): pp. 102–108, 202.

"Urban Vigor." *Architecture* (July 1991): pp. 42–44.

"The U.S. Embassy Office Building, Tokyo." *Architectural Record* (April 1977): pp. 101–106.

"The Utopian and the Pragmatic." Review of "Houses for Sale" exhibition. *ARTnews* (November 1980): pp. 14–15.

Venti Progetti per il Futuro del Lingotto. Milan: Etas Libri, 1984: pp. 136–143.

Vitta, Maurizio. "Una torre per la storia." *l'Arca* (Milan: February 1992): pp. 26–31.

Vreeland, Tim. "Tim Vreeland Interviews Cesar Pelli, Edgardo Contini and Allen Rubinstein" and "Pacific Design Center ...Its Aesthetic is Partly Intellectual, Partly Graphic." *L.A. Architect* (September 1975).

Watanabe, Hiroshi. "Evaluation: America's Presence in Tokyo—A Japanese Viewpoint." *Architecture* (July 1984): pp. 75–81.

Wiseman, Carter. "Cesar Pelli." *New York* (September 20, 1982): pp. 86–87.

Wiseman, Carter. "Room at the Tops" *New York* (December 21, 1981) pp. 64–66.

Wiseman, Carter. "A Vision with a Message." *Architectural Record* (March 1987): pp. 112–121.

Wiseman, Carter. "The Next Great Place: The Triumph of Battery Park City." *New York* (June 16, 1986): pp. 34–41.

Wolner, Edward W. "Urban Icon." *Inland Architect* (January/February 1990): pp. 44–48.

"World Financial Center." *Nikkei Architecture* (Tokyo, September 1985): pp. 74–83.

"World Financial Center and Battery Park City." *Nikkei Architecture* (Tokyo, September 1988): pp. 70–113.

"The World Financial Center, New York, New York." *Architectural Design* (London, January/February 1985): pp. 32–35.

World Residential Design. Tokyo: Dai Nippon N.I.C. Ltd, 1991, plates 501–509.

Yamashita, Tsukasa. "Eero Saarinen and His Works: Interviewee #4, Cesar Pelli." *A + U* (Tokyo, April 1984 extra edition): pp. 198–203.

Yee, Roger. "The Capture of the Sun in California." *Progressive Architecture* (December 1974): pp. 94–99.

Zobl, Engelbert. "Herring Hall." *Architektur Aktuell* (Berlin, April 1987): pp. 60–62.

Zobl, Engelbert. "World Financial Center." *Architektur Aktuell* (Berlin, April 1987): pp. 62–64.

Acknowledgments

I would like to thank my partners Fred Clarke and Rafael Pelli, and all the architects and designers at Cesar Pelli & Associates.

I would also like to thank the clients, associate architects, consultants and others who helped make the projects featured in this monograph a reality.

My thanks to Mariko Masuoka and Philip Koether, who reviewed the images and layouts of each project. Also to Jack Gold, who wrote the descriptions of every project in the book, and prepared captions and photographic credits; and to Bernard Proeschl who organized the mailing of photographs and slides to Australia.

Photography Credits

Photographer: Peter Aaron, Esto Photographics: 54 (1); 55 (2); 188 (5); 189 (8,9); 191 (12); 195 (9); 196 (10); 197 (11–13).

Photographer: Joe C. Aker, Aker/Burnette, Inc.: 34 (1); 36 (9); 37 (10–12).

Photographer: Robert Benson: 137 (bottom right); 160 (2); 161 (3); 162 (4); 163 (6); 164 (10–11); 165 (12); 172 (1); 174 (3,5,6); 175 (7); 190 (11).

Photographer: Stephen L. Bergerson: 48 (2).

Renderer: J. Bunton, Cesar Pelli & Associates: 210 (51–530.

Renderer: William Butler, Cesar Pelli & Associates: 140 (5,6): with Robert Narracci: 118 (1); 222 (21); rendered photograph: 225 (28).

Photographer: Carolina Photo Group: 68 (12).

Photographer: Kenneth Champlin: 21 (bottom right); 82 (1); 83 (3); 85 (bottom right); 103 (3); 104 (4); 106 (9); 108 (1,2); 115 (22,23,24); 126 (1); 127 (3); 186 (1); 211 (4–5); 216 (6); 217 (9).

Renderer: David Chen, Cesar Pelli & Associates: 220 (19); 221 (20).

Photographer: John Connell: 85 (bottom left); 98 (1,2); 99 (3); 100 (4); 101 (8).

Photographer: Alan Delaney: 93 (11).

Renderer: Turan Duda, Cesar Pelli & Associates: 121 (5).

Photographer: Jeff Goldberg, Esto Photographics: 3 (bottom right); 137 (top left and right); 167 (2); 168 (4); 170 (7,10); 171 (12); 192 (2); 193 (3,4); 195 (9); 196 (10); 197 (11,12,13).

Photographer: Arthur Golding: 24 (1).

Renderer: Michael Green, Cesar Pelli & Associates: 111 (9).

Photographer: Tim Griffith, Images Australia Pty. Ltd.: 65 (4); 67 (9,11); 69 (13); 74 (4,5); 75 (8); 205 (9,10); 206 (11); 208 (16,17).

Photographer: John Grossman: 138 (2).

Renderer: Kristin Hawkins, Cesar Pelli & Associates: 183 (4).

Photographer: Paul Hester: 39 (5); 40 (8); 41 (9); 137 (bottom left); 140 (4); 141 (10); 143 (14); 144 (1); 145 (3); 146 (4); 147 (8,9).

Photographer: Stephen Hill: 87 (3).

Photographer: Robin Holland: 61 (13).

Photographer: Wolfgang Hoyt: 76 (1).

Photographer: Greg Hursley, R. Greg Hursley, Inc.: 139 (3); 142 (13); 143 (15,16).

Photographer: Timothy Hursley, The Arkansas Office: 3 (bottom left); 21 (top right); 56 (5); 57 (7); 59 (9); 63 (16,17); 64 (3); 66 (5); 67 (10,11); 70 (15); 71 (16); 149 (3); 150 (4); 151 (5,6); 153 (3); 154 (5); 155 (7); 156 (8,9); 158 (12,13); 159 (15); 177 (3,4); 178 (5–7); 180 (13,14); 181 (16,17); 206 (12); 207 (13,14); 204 (7,8); 208 (15); 209 (18).

Renderer: Hiroyuki Kataoka, Cesar Pelli & Associates: 78 (1); 152 (1); 187 (3); 194 (8).

Photographer: Balthazar Korab, Balthazar Korab Ltd. Photography: 21 (bottom left); 22 (1); 23 (4); 26 (1,2); 27 (4); 32 (1); 33 (2); 43 (bottom right); 46 (3); 47 (4).

Photographer: Balthazar and Christian Korab, Balthazar Korab Ltd. Photography: 43 (bottom left); 48 (3); 49 (4); 50 (5,6); 51 (9); 52 (10–12); 53 (13).

Photographer: Mark Lohman: 97 (8).

Renderer: Anthony Markese, Cesar Pelli & Associates: 109 (5); 112 (11); with Barbara Endres: 113 (16).

Photographer: Peter Mauss, Esto Photographics: 31 (4); 60 (11).

Photographer: Norman McGrath: 29 (3–5).

Photographer: Courtesy Metropolitan Washington Airports Authority Archives: 111 (10).

Photographer: John S. Miller, John Stuart Miller Photography: 89 (3).

Photographer: Jon Miller, Hedrich-Blessing Photographers: 79 (4); 80 (5–8); 81 (9).

Renderer: Jun Mitsui, Cesar Pelli & Associates: 46 (1).

Photographer: Rita Nannini: 60 (12).

Renderer: Robert Narracci, Cesar Pelli & Associates: 119 (2); 173 (2).

Renderer: Steve Oles: 88 (1).

Photographer: Cesar Pelli: 3 (top left); Cesar Pelli at Gruen Associates: 3 (top right); 21 (top left); 26 (3); 43 (top left); 45 (3).

Photographer: Cesar Pelli & Associates: 9; 10; 12; 13; 14; 16; 89 (2); 93 (12); 109 (3–5); 111 (9); 112 (11); tip ins (12–15); 113 (16); 114 (18,19); 115 (22–24); 116 (25,26); 117 (27–32); 118 (1); 119 (2); 126 (1,2); 128 (4,5); 131 (9,10); 132 (11); 133 (14–17); 134 (18,19); 190 (10,11); 211 (3,4); 212 (6–8); 215 (3–5); 217 (10); 223 (23,24); 224 (25); 225 (27); back cover.

Renderer: Cesar Pelli at Gruen Associates: 45 (4).

Photographer: Richard Payne: 73 (3); 74 (6,7).

Photographer: Jeff Perkell: cover; 43 (top right); 56 (6).

Photographer: Cervin Robinson: 30 (1); 31 (3,5).

Renderer: Michael Sechman, Michael Sechman Associates: 123 (7); 124 (8); 201 (8).

Photographer: Peter Sutherland: 85 (top right); 95 (3); 96 (4,5,7).

Photographer: Courtesy Takenaka Corporation: 214 (2).

Photographer: Nick Wheeler: 175 (6).

Index

Bold page numbers refer
to projects included in
Selected and Current Works.